Long March, Short Spring

Long March, Short Spring

The Student Uprising at Home and Abroad

by Barbara and John
Ehrenreich

New York and London

LA
186
E35

To the Vietnamese people

Preface

We spent most of the early part of the spring of 1968 trying to figure out how to get away from school (graduate school). Then sometime between April 23 (during the Columbia uprising) and May 10 (the night of the barricades in Paris) we decided that universities might be more interesting than we'd realized. Many other people in the American student movement were beginning to feel the same way. Up to then our international interests had focused on Vietnam and Latin America. We knew a lot about the N.L.F., the Huks in the Philippines, and the Guatemalan guerrillas, but hardly anything about our European counterparts: SDS in Germany, the March 22nd Movement in France, the Italian movement. When the universities blew up in the spring, we decided to find out about these student movements.

We flew to Europe to get there before schools were out for the summer. Although there wasn't much time, we managed to find plenty of people to talk to. We had no special desire to meet the "leaders" of the movements, but usually ended up meeting them anyway. We did our best to talk to as many ordinary students as we could. In several countries, we got a lot of help from American friends who have been living there. They filled us in on what was going on and made sure we met plenty of people. Since we've been back in New York, the flow has been in the other direction: many European students have come through, brought us up to date, and actually helped write the book—by reading drafts, criticizing, and discussing interpretations.

This is not an "objective" book (is there such a thing anyway?). We are not reporters. We did not simply interview people; we asked questions and we argued. We spent more time discussing strategy and common problems than we did making notes. Of course, we have even less detachment about the events described in the Columbia chapter. We, or friends of ours, were at Columbia at many times during the struggle as participants.

This is also not a comprehensive book. There is nothing in it about the important movements in Japan or Mexico, or about any of the smaller movements which are springing up in almost every capitalist country and in a few Communist countries. It is about only four countries besides the United States: England, France, Germany, and Italy. Even within these narrow limits, we didn't try to be complete. We tried to keep within the limits of what we knew from first-hand accounts. So the chapter on Germany centers on the movement in Frankfurt and Berlin. The chapter on Italy is about Turin and Rome. These are the key cities for the movements in the two countries; they were also the only cities we visited in Germany and Italy. The chapter on England is short partly because our visit there was short.

The emphasis varies from country to country (that is, from chapter to chapter). In Germany, we were most interested in how the movement has developed over the last five years in the context of the country's history. In France, we emphasize the subject we discussed continually with French students: the dynamics of revolutionary change and its meaning for revolutionary organization. Also, we stick to the *student* role in May; the full story of the workers' role is beyond the scope of this book. The Italian chapter stresses university problems, as the Italians did. England is included not because it has a mighty movement (it doesn't yet) but for the insights it gave us into how universities produce radical students.

The chapter on the American movement is the least balanced of all. It's not just about one city, but about one university, Columbia. Other people have written histories of the American New Left (see bibliography). We think Columbia summarizes much of what the American New Left movement has been about for the last five years: many lines of development converge on Morningside Heights. More important, the Columbia experience seems to point the way to new directions for the American movement, so it is important to understand in detail what happened there.

* * *

History we leave to the historians. We were interested in *experience,* so it could become part of our (and your) experience. The people who shared their experience with us spent hours and days at it, so in a way, the book is really a collective effort. To mention everyone involved by name would fill a whole chapter. But we would like to acknowledge a few people who went out of their way to help.

In England, we relied on two American friends, Jon Schwartz and Alan Steinbach, and an Englishman, Mike Rustin.

In France, an American, Dick Howard, provided us with indispensable orientation in a very confusing situation and introduced us to many French students. We also thank Daniel Guérin and Fabrice, Hervé, Jean, Matthias, Catherin, Helen, Daniel, Lion, François, and Danielle.

In Rome, we thank Enzo Modugno, Giovanni Graziani,

Luca Meldolesi, Nicolette Stamme, and Beatrice. In Turin, we thank Luigi and Laura Bobbio, Pepino and Mario.

In Germany, we thank Rainer Deppe, Rainer Roth, Frank Wolff, Lothar Menne, Heinz Meier, Bernd Rabehl, Hartmut Hausserman, Walter Weller, Sigrid Fronius, and especially Uwe Bergmann and Maria Siegemund.

Finally, in New York, at Columbia, we thank Mark Rudd, Josh De Wind, Josie Duke, Dave Gilbert, and Beth Reisen.

Needless to say, none of these people are responsible for errors, either factual or in interpretation. If anyone besides us is responsible for the interpretations, it is our friends in the movement, with whom we've talked things over for years.

Finally, Paul Sweezy and Leo Huberman are responsible for suggesting that we write this book. Over the last few years we have learned much from both of them.

BARBARA AND JOHN EHRENREICH

New York City
November, 1968

Contents

Long March, Short Spring

CHAPTER ONE

The Year of the Student

*Something is happening here
and you don't know what it is,
do you, Mr. Jones?*
—Bob Dylan

1968: the year of the Revolutionary Student.

March: in Rome thousands of students fought an all-day battle with the police in the Valle Giulia.

April: in West Germany thousands of students blockaded newspaper publishing plants and burned the newspapers. In New York the Tactical Police Force battled for three hours to recapture Columbia University from its students.

May: 40,000 students and workers turned out for Berlin's biggest May Day demonstration in three decades. Paris saw the fiercest street-fighting since the Liberation. Students barricaded the streets of the Latin Quarter and fought the police all night, setting off a massive general strike that almost brought down the government. Throughout West Germany, students disrupted the universities to protest the government's new emergency laws.

June: students in Brussels, Stockholm, Amsterdam, Tokyo, and London occupied their schools or met the police on the streets.

As we write this in September, Mexican students and police are clashing in the heaviest fighting since the Revolution.

In the spring of 1968, revolutionary student movements emerged in almost every major country in the "Free World." No one had any reason to expect it. For twenty years European and North American governments had faced only the feeblest domestic radicalism. Europe had not only recovered from the war, but was far more stable and prosperous than it had ever been before. In the United States, obesity seemed to be well ahead of malnutrition as a major health problem. Everywhere unemployment was low. Workers were buying cars, television sets, washing machines, and camping equipment. The traditional Marxist predictions of the impoverishment of the working class and the collapse of capitalism sounded quaintly anachronistic. What could class struggle mean in the modern "classless" societies? Liberal savants applauded "the end of ideology." This was the age of reform. No social problem was too great to be solved by minor technical adjustments in the socio-political machinery. Revolutions might tear through the underdeveloped world, for, as everyone knows, Communism thrives on poverty. But the danger to the advanced countries was over.

Until the spring of 1968. When it came, no government was prepared with an answer or an excuse. Liberal journalists theorized about a "generation gap," but couldn't explain why youth should have gone to the left. Maybe things were just too comfortable and young people were feeling guilty about their soft lives. According to university officials, most students were still as wholesome as ever, except for the tiny bands of terrorists who disrupted one university and then dashed off to stir up another.

In fact, it was a mass movement. In Berlin the majority of the Free University's 15,000 students are seasoned demonstrators. In France the movement may have started in March with a few hundred partisans, but by May it numbered in the millions. The United States had never had a mass radical movement anything like the European communist movements, but the 1960's showed it wasn't immune. Berkeley led the way, and by 1968 the American movement was large and experienced enough to have exported the words "sit-in" and "direct action" to radicals all over the world. In May, six thousand students went on strike at Columbia University. Later in the summer 10,000 students and ex-students converged on downtown Chicago to stain the Democratic Convention with their blood.

The movement had been large, if not really massive, before the spring of 1968. People were getting used to the sight of thousands of students marching, picketing or rallying. But in the spring of 1968 the movement wasn't only massive, it was violent. Crowds didn't march, they practiced "mobile street tactics." Demonstrations led regularly to battles with the police. In Germany the spring demonstrations against the newspaper monopoly ended with two dead and hundreds injured. In Rome students fought off police attacks literally with sticks and stones. In Paris students burned cars and threw Molotov cocktails and paving stones to defend themselves from the cops' barrages of tear gas and concussion grenades. American students have always been much tamer than Europeans. But when cops invaded Columbia in mid-May, students fought back with showers of Coke bottles and ashtrays. Even in peaceful England, a spring anti-war demonstration climaxed in hand-to-hand combat with the police.

There have been massive and even violent left movements in Western capitalist countries before. From a historical point of view, perhaps the strangest feature of the new radicalism was the new radicals themselves. They weren't underpaid or unemployed workers. They were ordinary middle-class kids. All of classical revolutionary theory, all the experience of past left movements, seemed to say that poverty and exploitation were what revolutions are all about, and that only the industrial workers or the peasants can show the way. In 1968 the people who took to the streets were fresh out of comfortable homes and seemed well on their way to respectable, well-paying professions. At first French workers laughed them off as "papa's boys." The press compared the early disturbances to dormitory beer brawls or panty raids. But there was a disturbing new ring to the chants that echoed throughout Europe and the United States: anti-authoritarian, anti-imperialist, and anti-capitalist. (Sometimes the tune *was* a little like a college football cheer: "Ho, Ho, Ho Chi Minh; the NLF is going to win" and "One, two, three, four—we don't want your dirty war. Five, six, seven, eight—we don't want your fascist state.")

In many countries the students soon found allies in the working class. In France the workers joined in *en masse*. In the United States the first signs of real black-white alliance are on the far militant side of the student movement. Even in conservative West Germany, thousands of young workers have demonstrated side by side with the students.

In September, as schools got ready for the second bout, what the students *might* do was front page news all over the Western world. Students began to compete with Negroes for the two-bit sociology features of national picture magazines. Major newspapers ran articles revealing that Dany Cohn-Bendit, Rudi Dutschke, and Mark Rudd all ate, slept, and showed respect for their parents. But not everyone was intrigued by the students for their colorful personalities. After Chicago, American liberals agonized over whether the students who had been "clean for Gene" would start to lose faith in "the system." Powerful American corporation leaders invited students to conferences and intimate chats to talk out "what the students really want." Students who seemed suitably "constructive" were rewarded with foundation grants to figure out how to "restructure" the university.

Co-optation and personalization by the press are only a part of the arsenal of beleaguered states. The other weapon is repression. When governments are nervous, they use repression. In 1968 they seemed to be nervous about movements which were unarmed, amorphous, and resolutely open-to-the-public. Trumped-up charges of drug use, inciting to riot, and even conspiracy to commit murder were being pressed against student leaders.

A new specter was haunting Europe, and America. It was no longer the specter of organized communism. The Communists had settled down, content to struggle for a few percentage points per election. In 1968 it was revolutionary students. In the United States, the theme of the presidential election was "law and order," which is the going euphemism for repression of blacks and students. For once, J. Edgar Hoover forgot about the communist threat long enough to point out the new "student threat." In France, de Gaulle spent the summer rounding up stray student radicals. And in West Germany and Italy, some student activists were beginning to face the possibility of having to go underground. But most students refused to let the threats of repression change their style. It wasn't they who were frightened.

CHAPTER TWO

What the Students Really Want

*Until our most fantastic demands are met, fantasy will be
at war with society. Society will attempt the suppression
of fantasy, but fantasy will spring up again and again,
infecting the youth, waging urban guerrilla warfare, sabotaging
the smooth functioning of bureaucracies, waylaying the
typist on her way to the watercooler, kidnapping the
executive between office and home, creeping into the bed-
rooms of respectable families, hiding in the chambers of
high office, gradually tightening its control, eventually
emerging into the streets, waging pitched battles and
winning (its victory is inevitable).*

*We are the vanguard of fantasy
Where we live is liberated territory in which fantasy moves
About freely at all hours of the day, from which it mounts
Its attacks on occupied territory.
Each day brings new areas under our control
Each day a new victory is reported
Each day fantasy discovers new forms of organization
Each day it further consolidates its control, has less to
Fear, can afford to spend more time in self discovery . . .
Even in the midst of battles it plans the cities of the future.*

*We are full of optimism .
We are the future*

Up Against the Wall/Motherfuckers
(a radical group in New York City)

CHAPTER THREE

Germany: The Long March

April 12, 1968: Tens of thousands of West Germans went to work without a newspaper. The news (if they could have found a newspaper to read) was this: Thousands of students were battling police to stop the giant newspaper publishing firm of Axel Springer from distributing its papers. Munich: two dead. Berlin: machine guns and barbed wire were going up around Springer headquarters. Springer was besieged by his own favorite scandal item—students. These events, which seemed to break out so suddenly, shouldn't have surprised anyone. They were the culmination of several years of development of a radical student movement, which in turn grew out of developments in Germany over the last decade.

The West Germany of the 1950's and early 1960's was the West Germany of "the miracle." The "new" capitalism, with its clever new mechanisms for preventing depressions, seemed to ensure economic and political stability. But in the early 1960's the rate of economic growth slowed down. Then in 1966, the impossible happened—the slowdown turned into a serious recession. In response to the slowdown of business, employers laid off thousands of men, and cut the wages of thousands more. The workers responded with strikes and slowdowns, which added up to the most serious labor unrest of the post-war period. By mid-1966, both government and industry realized the necessity of serious measures to combat the recession and curb labor unrest. But the

government in power was identified with the economic policies which had led up to the decline. The measures that would
have to be taken were likely to be as unpopular as the decline itself, and a large opposition party waited in the wings.
The obvious way to prevent any serious threat to the new
government measures was to absorb the opposition into the
government. And so, in December 1966, the two major parties—the Christian Democrats, who had governed Germany
since the war, and the Social Democrats, heirs of the socialist
tradition and party of the workers—joined together in a
"Grand Coalition."

The Grand Coalition was a grand success. An austerity
budget was introduced, without, of course, much parliamentary opposition. Taxes were raised. Government spending was cut, including spending on various social security
measures, subsidies to certain branches of industry, and military spending. Finally, after a decade's discussion, laws giv-
ing the government great powers in the event of an "emergency" (to be declared by the government) were reintro-
duced into parliament. The Grand Coalition also accelerated
political trends which had started over a decade ago. The in-
corporation of the only major opposition party into the ruling government signified that political parties meant less and
less. Parliament itself was ceasing to be the arena in which
real clashes of interest were resolved, in which real decision-
making occurred. Instead, the executive of an increasingly
bureaucratic and authoritarian state became the center of
power, as all the traditional mechanisms of opposition to
that power declined.

The mid-1960's also saw the emergence of a crisis in the
universities, a crisis intimately linked to the changes in the
economy. The rapid growth of the economy and the development of the high technology and the sales effort character-

istic of an advanced capitalist industrial economy had led to a growing need for a variety of highly educated workers. Teachers, engineers, chemists, advertising men, computer programmers, etc.—all were in demand, and the university would have to supply them. But the university was neither ready nor willing. It had been designed to train an elite for nineteenth-century professions, not a mass for twentieth-century jobs. By the mid-1960's, the crisis was evident. The universities were overcrowded. The curriculum was obsolete, and the professors, all-powerful in German universities since the nineteenth century, were closing ranks against any modernization.

The crisis hit just at the time when it was least possible to do anything serious about it. The government, in the midst of an austerity program, was not about to undertake any vast expansion of the educational system. The government's only alternative was to attack the problems of the university with administrative measures, measures aimed at tightening up the slack in the educational system. Thus, many local governments sought to limit enrollment at local universities by raising the entrance fees. In addition, they proposed limiting the time a student could spend at the university to eight semesters, cutting down on the many students who, for economic or psychological reasons, attended part time, and cutting down on the students who, in the interests of a broad education, leisurely waded through ten or twelve semesters of schooling. (Almost half of the students took more than ten semesters to complete their university work.) To the students, this might be efficiency but it was not "progress." It sacrificed the economic and psychological needs of the students to the needs of business for a cheap, "efficient" university. It did not attempt a basic solution to the university crisis.

If West Germany as a whole had problems in the mid-sixties, so did West Berlin—only sooner and worse. Berlin was the show window of West Germany, the living demonstration of the virtues of capitalism. All of the attitudes of West Germany toward capitalism, communism, and democracy were mirrored, even caricatured in West Berlin. But if its attitudes and style were more intense than those of Germany, its problems were, too. West Berlin was, in fact, an empty show window. Built up in hectic spurts of American largesse, the economy of this city without a country became increasingly irrational. Industries were unwilling to invest in the uncertain future of the "island city." The only investments drawn to the city by the tax incentives of the West German government were speculative enterprises where rapid tax write-offs meant rapid profits. Berlin went through a dazzling but hollow boom in expensive housing, offices, and hotels. The workers of Berlin, especially young workers, were the first to notice that Berlin was going nowhere. Wages were higher in West Germany, and jobs more plentiful. They left by the thousands, leaving Berlin a city of the old. Twenty-two per cent of the population is over sixty-five (almost double the figure for West Germany as a whole).

Just as Berlin was a showpiece, so was its university. In 1948, with the Soviet blockade of Berlin underway and the cold war freeze setting in, the Free University of Berlin was founded. To the students, who took the lead in founding it, the Free University was an alternative to the arbitrary and authoritarian Humboldt University in East Berlin. To young, liberal, anti-Communist and anti-fascist teachers, it was a chance to create a new model of a democratic university, a clear departure from the old, professor-dominated German model. To the West Germans and to the Americans, it was another propaganda weapon, a demonstration of the generous new democracy of the West.

As a result of these pressures, the Free University of Berlin was, indeed, unique among German universities: it did give the students a role in university decision-making. For example, the university senate was made up of two faculty representatives from each faculty of the university, the rector and vice-rector, and two representatives of the student body. There was also representation of the students within the individual faculties. This minority representation may sound trivial, but psychologically it was important. In fact, until 1958, there was never an occasion on which the students and the professors in the senate split. In the early 1950's, the Free University was a successful experiment; students and faculty alike felt they had created a new kind of university.

But by the late fifties, the democratic consensus was beginning to wear a little thin. For one thing, unlike in 1948, there were so many students that the university didn't have to worry about attracting new ones or catering to the ones it had. Even if they'd tried to preserve the democratic image, the mechanisms that had assured democracy in a small school were inadequate for a large one. Second, the experiment had been a success and the university had become respectable. Professors who were less adventurous, less liberal, and more traditional than the early professors began to come to Berlin. They were not in the slightest interested in the new model university. Finally, the students, too, had changed. This was a post-war generation, less interested in fighting the ideological battles of their fathers than in fulfilling new and higher expectations of democracy and freedom. As a result of these changes, by the early sixties, the much vaunted freedom and democracy that the "Berlin model" offered students was

less and less real. Meanwhile, the Berlin university was subject to the same kinds of pressures as other West German universities: overcrowding, out-of-date curriculum, and government reforms that did not concern themselves with the students' immediate interests.

* * *

Now it is easy enough to write what happened. Far more
interesting than just what happened is what it meant to the
people it was happening to. Events do not unfold in people's minds in the linear, straightforward style of a history
text. Sometimes many events pile up in people's consciousness before a single one of them can be understood. The transformation of West German students from anti-Communist
liberals to revolutionary socialists did not proceed at the
same even pace as the deterioration of West German democracy. All we can do now is try (with the insights of some German sociology students) to reconstruct how each political-
economic development fed into the growing disenchantment
of the students. Most of what follows is about Berlin, since
that's where the German student movement began.

First there was the development of West German politics.
Remember that if you were about twenty years old in 1960,
then your father was probably about thirty in 1940. For
many German students in the early 1960's, the overriding
experience of adolescence was the discovery of their fathers'
past. Their fervor for democracy, unlike many Americans',
was fed on guilt and horror, not nationalism. To these liberal students, who couldn't have cared less about the government's goal of "efficiency," the Grand Coalition came as a
special shock. Their hopes for legal, peaceful change vanished
along with the parliamentary opposition. The erosion of

democracy was made doubly sinister by two other events in the early '60's. First, Germany was once again rearming; and second, many former Nazis were crawling out from obscurity and into positions of wealth and power. With sickened fascination, some young intellectuals researched out the pre-war and wartime experiences of prominent contemporary Germans. One student told us how, as an athletic and apolitical teenager, he had assisted in this kind of research, and slowly pieced together the function of the "camp" outside of town and the former career of a best friend's father. Such studies did not automatically produce radicals, but they contributed to the education of a generation which literally *cannot* trust anyone over forty.

Second, the economy was faltering. The Berlin showpiece was turning out to be tinsel; the German miracle was becoming a charlatan's trick. At the same time, the East German economy, which had served for so long as proof that only capitalism could ensure economic growth, was gaining steadily upon that of the Western zone, overtaking it in many areas such as education and even in some areas of production. Every modern building that rose in the East undercut the faith the students had been raised in, that only capitalism could guarantee prosperity, and with it social stability. By 1965, you didn't have to be too perceptive to notice the new mood in the university. Eleanor Dulles, the sister of former U.S. Secretary of State John Foster Dulles and of former CIA director Allen Dulles, interpreted it this way: "The students of Berlin are restless. They want to break through the barriers, extend the field of their experience, travel in the East, explore the ideas and know the theories of the Communists."

Third, by 1963, the thaw in the cold war was setting in. Russia and the United States were getting almost cordial.

This was confusing to Berliners of all ages. Wasn't the U.S. their sole protection, and Berlin, in turn, the courageous, easternmost outpost of Free Europe? To the students it was downright sinister. What was to stop the United States from dropping Berlin to please its new-found friend? When you came right down to it, the walled city was an American pawn. This understanding led some of the more political students to review their post-war German history. When they did so, they concluded, as some American scholars have too, that the West (America in particular) shares a large part of the guilt for the plight of Germany, up to and including the building of the Berlin Wall. The myth of Germany beset by an external enemy gave way before the realization of the duplicity of the Bonn and Berlin governments and of their democratic protector, the United States. Students' critical energies, which up to now had been occupied with the critique of Communism, turned toward the problems of the capitalist world.

Fourth, the struggles in the third world became more intense in the late fifties and early sixties. One after another, the democratic capitalist countries revealed the brutality hidden behind the mask of democratic affluence. 1958-62: France, in Algeria. 1960: England, France, Belgium, in the Congo. 1961 and again in 1962: the U.S. in Cuba. And especially, crucially, 1964 and after, the United States in Vietnam. Capitalism had bared its teeth. One could no longer believe that the capitalist countries, especially the most important one and the one most important to Germany, the United States, still represented the ideals of peace, democracy, and justice. "Democracy and murder are not mutually exclusive" said one early anti-Vietnam poster in Berlin.

Finally, in our list of developments disillusioning the students, there was the university. The university had not been exempt from the general deterioration of democratic institutions. Overcrowded and impersonal, it was less and less satisfying as a refuge for students disgusted by the brutality of the outside world. In Berlin especially, where the students supposedly had a share of power, the more activist and idealistic students discovered that in fact they had no power. The faculty and the administration could overrule them at every turn.

* * *

Of course, the Berlin students did not just sit and watch these changes in the university and in society. As they grew more and more disillusioned, they began to undertake little actions of one sort or another. But every foray into action seemed to pay off only in more firmly entrenched disillusionment. In 1964 the liberals and leftists pulled themselves together for a vigorous campaign on student issues. It worked; they won for the first time a clear majority in the student parliament. Once in power, the liberals quickly learned that the authorities were not the slightest bit interested in their proposals for university reform. The newly elected parliamentarians found themselves under increasing pressure from their constituency for more militant action.

The following year brought two important tests of student powerlessness. Civil liberties had been among the first of the post-war luxuries to be sacrificed by the Free University in the interests of rational expansion. The students began to find this out when in May 1965 they invited a left-liberal journalist, Erich Kuby, to speak at the university. No, said the administration, Kuby has been banned from speaking on campus since the last time he expressed his "too radical" views, two years ago. Indignantly, the students went ahead and held

the meeting at the Technical University of Berlin, which
had not had the foresight to ban Kuby earlier. Later that
summer, Ekkehart Krippendorff, an assistant at the Free University, discovered he was out of a job. He had written an
article attacking the Free University's rector for barring the
philosopher Karl Jaspers from speaking. A protest meeting
organized by the student government attracted seven hundred students. These two events, the "Krippendorff case"
and the "Kuby case" directly insulted the increasingly liberal
student body and gave rise to the first mass assemblies on university problems.

Perhaps the students wouldn't have gone much further
than leaflets and meetings if university problems had been
the only issue. But by 1964 and 1965, Vietnam had begun
to overshadow local problems. The early West German
demonstrations against the war, like the early demonstrations
in the United States, were entirely legal, with permits and
police-approved routes of march. The students also held conferences on Vietnam, hoping that by simply presenting the
truth, they could arouse the rest of the population. But no-
body, including the press, paid any attention. Anti-imperialist
demonstrations became more frequent and more vigorous.
In December 1964, a thousand students demonstrated against
Congolese Premier Tshombe when he visited Berlin. Two
months later, a similar number demonstrated against a
South African exhibit in Berlin. A few days after the demonstration, the United States began the bombing of North Vietnam. Outraged, the students began to feel that such barbar-
ity called for something more than peaceful, legal protest.

Students had been following the growth of an increasingly
militant anti-war movement in the United States. They had
read about the direct action techniques of the civil rights
movement in the American South. Now, the urgency of the

war in Vietnam seemed to demand direct action in Germany. There was no other way to confront the public with the full horror of the war, to force them to face the issues and to decide which side they were on. There was no other way to break through the newspapers' wall of silence and force people to pay attention. There was no other alternative to the impotent, bureaucratic protests of the student union and the adult pacifist groups. By February 1966, student demonstrations against the war were leading regularly to clashes with the police.

The West German student movement was underway. The gap between the ideals of the students and the reality of West German society had grown too wide to be bridged by peaceful negotiation. Students could no longer equate capitalism and democracy, communism and totalitarianism. Representational methods, in the university and in the society, had been tested and found useless. The model nation of the world, the United States, was displaying the bestiality that students identified with Nazi Germany. Western "democracy," domestically, in foreign policy, and in the university, was essentially authoritarian. Decisions were not made by the people whose lives they affected, but by small and distant elites. These understandings were confirmed by every action the students undertook, and, with every action, more and more students were dislodged from passivity and apathy. Once started, the movement followed its own logic, meeting resistance with greater militance, repression with deeper conviction.

* * *

Many student groups, from the young Protestant alliance to the student union (AStA) swung to the left in the last few years. But none moved so far and so fast as SDS (*Sozialis-tischer Deutscher Studentenbund*), which now dominates the West German student movement. (In Berlin, SDS even controls the student government.)

SDS began as the youth group of the German Social Democratic Party (SPD). But it moved to the left as its parent group moved to the right. In 1961, the SPD and SDS split. In its early period of independent existence, from 1961 to 1964, SDS was little more than a set of loosely coordinated study groups. This three-year period of study is in large part responsible for the theoretical sophistication for which SDS is now famous among student movements. Most of the theoretical work was on problems of Marxist theory—imperialism, etc. The major specific analysis of an institution came in the form of some very detailed work on the university, culminating in a paper entitled "The University in a Democratic Society." This paper concluded, among other things, that it was impossible to have a democratic university in an undemocratic society.

Especially important during these formative years of SDS was the so-called "Frankfurt School" of sociologists. This group of sociologists—Max Horkheimer, Theodore Adorno, and Jürgen Habermas—were, to the students, the bearers of the Marxist tradition in sociology. It was from an exiled member of the Frankfurt School, Herbert Marcuse, that the students learned their most important lessons: Repression in advanced capitalist societies is not just a matter of police and courts. It is inherent in all the institutions of society. In schools and the way people learn to think, in cultural institutions, in language itself, society limits its people and prevents them from realizing that there might be other ways of living. Only when someone breaks out of the internalized repressions and tries to change things, are overt measures like the police necessary. So in struggling against advanced capitalism, you have to carry the struggle into all the institutions of society, from the governmental apparatus to the movie industry. The struggle must concentrate on exposing the authoritarianism hidden in every institution. As people see the inherent violence of their society, they will glimpse the possibility of alternative societies. They will cease to be "one-dimensional"—so locked into the present that one cannot transcend it and see entirely different ways of doing things.

Marcuse believed that struggle could only be undertaken by a group which had somehow resisted total integration into the status quo. Students are such a "marginal" group. They are not yet tied down by jobs or a family, and (in their studies at least) are relatively free to critically examine their society. (For other reasons, American Negroes are also a marginal group.) To Marcuse, it is only among such marginal groups that opposition to the system has a chance of developing. Hence, his thinking was a justification and a theoretical basis for organizing students into radical struggle.

Though this prolonged period of study was productive, it was not always emotionally satisfying to the young radicals. Some groups of radicals insisted on action, even though at that time the majority of the students were not ready to join them. For example, one group outside of SDS (called "Viva Maria" after the Bardot-Moreau movie about the Mexican Revolution) undertook "provo actions" against such targets as a national convention of advertising men.

Not that they believed these actions could achieve anything; the source of revolutionary energy, they maintained, could only be the third world. Germany was unshakeable. One of the early activists described the desperation of this period: "We felt like committing suicide." And when groups like these decided to act in earnest, it was still not because they rationally believed they could change things. It was rather, as prominent SDS'er Rudi Dutschke later said (he had been a member of Viva Maria) an existential decision: "No abstract theory of history holds us together, only existential nausea at a society which chatters about freedom, about the immediate interests and needs of the individual, while it subtly and brutally prevents the socio-economic emancipation of a struggling people."

By 1964, however, more and more of the SDS study groups were turning to action. We have described above some of the early demonstrations on Vietnam and other issues, and the agitations within the university for civil liberties. As student discontent and frustration grew, the example of direct action as practiced in America became more and more persuasive. As the students themselves became more and more disillusioned with the society, they came to believe that the whole society was full of unresolved tensions. Perhaps advanced countries like Germany were not, after all, revolution-proof. If they could bring the violence and authoritarianism of the society out into the open, they argued, people would shake loose from cultural and institutional repression in great numbers, and the movement would grow explosively. Direct action, forced confrontations—these were the tactics SDS would use to bring the latent violence out into the open.

The Berlin government obligingly provided an issue to test the students' growing militance. Early in 1966 the government had begun to toy with the idea of limiting students' stay at the university to eight semesters. In June, the Free University faculty met to discuss the proposal. The SDS-influenced student union, AStA, decided to abandon representational procedures and called for a general meeting of all students. Three thousand students showed up, and they decided not to petition, but to sit-in outside of the faculty meeting. (The word "sit-in" seems to be the same in all languages.) Although this first sit-in ended quietly enough, it was an important turning point: the beginning of a *mass* student movement. Thousands of students were asked to make a decision and thousands did. Of course, this first mass direct action had little bearing on the issues that really concerned the political vanguard, SDS. Students had moved because their own way of life was at stake. At this point most of the students still felt that SDS rhetoric went a little too far—that it bordered on violence.

As student militance spread to other fronts, there was less and less question about which side the violence lay on. In December 1966, two thousand students broke off from a larger peace demonstration and tried to march to the center of Berlin. On the way they were stopped—their first encounter with massive police violence. They had certainly not meant to provoke an attack, for they never expected the police to be so zealous about an issue so abstract (for Germany) as Vietnam. Then, in April 1967, Hubert Humphrey was scheduled to visit Berlin. The hippy fringe of SDS, the dozen or so members of "Commune 1," decided to greet Humphrey with a happening. They prepared a mock riot, complete with pudding grenades and smoke bombs, calculated to make Humphrey look as ridiculous as possible. The day before the visit, the police raided the Commune, arresting the communards, confiscating the pudding, and charging a serious plot to assassinate Humphrey. Newspapers ran banner headlines, "Humphrey's Life Threatened," although it was perfectly obvious from the nature of the evidence collected by the police that the whole thing was a joke. Nor did the press make any fine distinctions about the instigators; just "students" were to blame. For the first time, students found themselves lumped together as the target of the press's bad will.

For any students who still worried that SDS had terrorist tendencies, there was the spectacle of the whimsical communards sitting in jail, while Humphrey went home, free to contemplate mass murder in Vietnam.

Up to this point the movement was still confined largely to Berlin, and still involved at most a few thousand students. Then, in June 1967, the Shah of Iran visited Berlin. For the Berlin public, the visit was preceded by countless newspaper articles of the dashing monarch and his beautiful young wife. For the students, the visit was preceded by the publication of a book detailing the poverty and oppression of the commoners in Iran,* the Shah's play place. Meetings were held, denouncing the Shah's visit. On June 2, the Shah attended the Berlin opera. Thousands of students demonstrated, throwing eggs and tomatoes. Suddenly the demonstrators were attacked by a band of several hundred hired thugs. The police stood by and watched the fight, as students were beaten and clubbed. Finally the police intervened—not to break up the battle but to add their own blows to those of the thugs.

When the battle died down, a student, Benno Ohnesorg, was found dead on the street, shot in the head by a policeman. The policeman claimed Ohnesorg had pulled a knife, and the newspapers trumpeted the story of the terrorist student. But the stories of the police kept changing, and after four or five versions, the truth came out: Ohnesorg had been shot down in cold blood by a policeman (who was never punished for the act). Students all over Germany were outraged. Demonstrators filled the streets of dozens of cities. Shortly thereafter, a national meeting was held at Hanover to discuss the events of June 2 and to discuss how large numbers of students could effectively take action in response. Ten thou-

* *Iran: The New Imperialism in Action,* by Bahman Nirumand. Published by Rowohlt in Germany, this book has been brought out in an English translation by Monthly Review Press.

sand students, from all over Germany, attended. The movement had finally spread to the whole of West Germany.

The events surrounding the Shah's visit deeply influenced the struggle within the university. Thousands of students felt, for the first time, an urgency that superseded academic concerns. If the university wasn't relevant to the issues uncovered by the Shah's visit, then it simply wasn't relevant at all. On June 3, six thousand students gathered at the Free University to discuss the previous day's events and demanded that regular classes be suspended so that discussion could continue. For the next week, classes were, in fact, turned over to discussions: on the lies of the police, manipulation by the press, the emergency situation in Berlin, the general decline of democracy in Germany, and the *critical* function of the university.

But the students soon realized that if they wanted a university that would train them to think critically and to act politically, so that they might reinstate democracy in the university and in the society, then they would have to create it themselves. And so they created their own "critical university." This was not an institution outside of and parallel to the existing university, like the American "free universities." It was embedded within the existing university. It set as its aims the permanent critique and practical reform of the university; the expansion and intensification of political practice in newly created centers of action, in the existing student groups, and in mass groups such as the student council; and the preparation of students to be critical and politically active in the practice of their academic professions.

The critical university was an action project as well as an intellectual one. Students from a course on history would go into their official university lectures and question the professor, in order to expose the ideology implicit in the views he was presenting. Or they would, as a group, "go-in" to a lecture and demand that the professor debate. Or they would "go-in" to an examination and discuss its ideological content out loud in front of the students who were taking the exam. In this way they would both prevent the university from performing its old ideological role, and help students develop a new, critical understanding of their subject. The critical university was also oriented toward action outside the university. For example, a group studying Vietnam might initiate an action on Vietnam. A group doing research on imperialism or on urban problems would write a pamphlet to assist an on-going organizing project.

One target of the student demonstrators after the Shah of Iran affair was the press, which had attacked the students in print as viciously as the police had with clubs. The newspapers had an old vendetta against the students, dating back to 1964 and the days before any large, violent demonstrations had yet occurred. As the movement spread, the newspaper calumny redoubled. Students were "outsiders"; they were "terrorists." Students don't work; they are "lazy," they are "parasites." Students engage in "perverted sexual practices."

As student after student, both in Berlin and in Frankfurt, told us, students are a journalistic substitute for Jews. What made the newspaper campaign almost universal was the monopolization of the West German press by one publishing concern—Axel Springer Verlag. Springer controls 78% of the daily newspaper and magazine circulation of Berlin, 43% of the circulation of all West Germany. Non-Springer newspapers got on the bandwagon, but Springer always called the tune: students were "Communists" or "FU [Free University] Chinese."

And the public ate it up. Students found themselves as isolated as, thirty years ago, the Jews had been. For left and left-liberal students, it became a matter of survival, not just a theoretical concern, to make allies among other sectors of the population. Otherwise they were prime targets for a serious repression, which the public would not protest but actually welcome. As one part of the attempt to break out of isolation, SDS began to agitate against the Springer monopoly. But they were still too weak; the campaign seemed abstract even to other students.

The students soon received another lesson in the power of the Springer press. They had planned an international conference on Vietnam, to take place in Berlin in February 1968. The Springer press began a campaign against this "conspiracy to commit illegal deeds." The city government, feeling the tug of the strings pulled by Axel Springer, promptly banned the meetings. SDS defied the city. They gained the cooperation of the rector of the Technical University in Berlin who granted them permission to use some rooms for the conference. They also challenged the city ban in court. Much to everyone's surprise, the court supported the students, saying that the city's ban was illegal. The conference came and was attended by thousands of students from all over Europe. At the close of the meeting, the students poured out onto the streets in a celebration of their victory over the city's attempted repression. Twenty thousand students paraded with red banners and National Liberation Front flags held high. But the city government was not to be thwarted in expressing its hostility to the students. With the aid of the press, they organized a giant counter-demonstration the next week. Fifty thousand Berliners demonstrated their support of the war in Vietnam. Violent intimidation of students was the order of the day. A student who resembled SDS leader Rudi Dutschke had to be protected by the police from being beaten by passers-by. No doubt the counter-demonstration reflected the feelings of the population of Berlin as a whole more accurately than the student demonstration had. The students had already realized how the press manipulated public opinion. Now they saw, apprehensively, how far the press could go to *mobilize* public opinion.

The stage was now set for the movement to become a truly mass movement of students. Thousands of students were already active, and thousands more had been exposed over a period of months to SDS rhetoric, press hatred, and police brutality. On April 11, Rudi Dutschke was shot in the head. His would-be assassin was an admirer of Hitler and Napoleon, and one of many Springer readers convinced that Rudi Dutschke was public enemy number one. Spontaneously, tens of thousands of students all over West Germany descended on the Springer plants.

Not only SDS demonstrated; dozens of other youth groups, including the youth group of the Social Democratic Party (SDS's "successor"), joined in, becoming more militant every day. One SDS'er told us in July, 1968, that these groups were now "where SDS was a year ago."

The students demonstrating at the Springer plants demanded nothing less than the expropriation of Springer. The truth, they argued, must not be the private property of one man. And if the government wouldn't free the German press, the students would. They burned newspapers, overturned delivery trucks, and blocked distribution of the papers in the streets. Now it was one thing for SDS to *say* it was anti-authoritarian and for a free press. It was another thing to go out on the streets and *protest* against authoritarianism and monopoly. But to carry these ideals to their logical conclusion, to go out and commit *crimes* against private property: this was something altogether new. And it was not just SDS and a few other leftist groups this time. When Dutschke was shot, tens of thousands of students bypassed years of SDS anti-authoritarian theory and went straight for the nearest Springer outlet. Of course, police all over West Germany ran out to meet them. For weeks afterward, a heavy police guard ensured the delivery of the Springer papers.

Scarcely had the campaign against Springer died down when the so-called "emergency laws" came up for their final reading in parliament. The laws outlined the new powers the executive of the government could assume in the event of an "emergency" (which could be declared by the government, more or less at will). It would be empowered to conscript all adult men into civil defense units. It would be able to tap phones, open mail, restrict travel, and suspend civil liberties. It would be able to forbid political or anti-social strikes and to use troops against demonstrations and organized insurgents. These laws, reminiscent of the emergency laws which Hitler had used to make his assumption of dictatorial power entirely legal, seemed aimed both at the recent student demonstrators and at the strikers of the recession period (in the Ruhr, miners had paraded with red flags). Both students and unions responded.

But the unions had to be cautious in their opposition. Rank and file discontent with the proposed laws ran deep. If unleashed, it might sweep right by the bureaucracy and get completely out of control. In some areas, the workers did get as far as wildcat strikes. But in most places, opposition was channeled into peaceful rallies. The leaders gave long, legalistic speeches attacking the laws, and the workers would go home feeling they had done what they could.

More dangerous styles of protest and mass actions were left to the students. They organized demonstrations all over Germany, including a march of 70,000 people (students and workers) on the capital at Bonn. In many places, protests and marches led to street-fighting with the police. In almost every city with a university, the students occupied the buildings—both as a protest and as a practical measure—to secure a base for resistance. On May 25, 1968, the New York *Times* said: "Chaotic conditions were reported from most West German universities as students boycotted lectures and moved in to occupy halls and institutes for teach-ins."

The students hoped that they would be able to draw the workers into a common struggle against the emergency laws and then extend this alliance to other issues. Workers did come to teach-ins, and in some cases, students gained the right to address union rallies and union meetings. But the SDS'ers were unprepared. They had elaborate theories of capitalism, but they did not know how to translate them into terms that would make sense to the workers, into terms that suggested a way of organizing their understanding into action. As a result, most of these contacts have been lost, although some worker-student discussion groups which grew out of the anti-emergency law struggle still continue.

* * *

SDS has come a long way from the esoteric study groups of the early sixties. Today it is the center of a mass radical movement. It can mobilize sudden spurts of action; it can probably survive long interims of quieter work. All over West Germany there are permanent SDS offices, full-time staff, and hundreds of reliable, dues-paying members. Outside of these, there are many times more students who have come to think of SDS as "their" organization, whether or not they're actually members. In fact, when we asked whether someone was an SDS'er, we were often told something like: "I don't know who's *in* SDS. We're all in the 'anti-authoritarian camp.' " German SDS seemed to be about as heterogeneous as American SDS. From region to region, the emphasis varied from anti-authoritarianism (with some youth-cultural over-tones) to a narrower anti-capitalism and even to traditional Communism.

Some people complained about SDS's looseness and disor-ganization, its lack of ideological coherency. For what seemed to us to be an amazingly healthy movement (and this is no doubt a healthy sign in itself) all SDS'ers we talked to were sharply self-critical: "We're not doing anything; the move-ment is dead!" or, "What good is all our theory, if it doesn't tell us what to do?"

In fact, SDS does have serious problems now. In the space of one year it has come to lead a mass movement, but it is still a *student* movement. Whether the issue is Vietnam or the emergency laws, students alone can do little more than raise a fuss. Yet even their own issues—issues related to their lives as students—give them a direct personal stake in changes in the entire society. They feel that there can only be a fully democratic university in a fully democratic society, and that capitalism, however democratic in form, is inherently elitist, hierarchical, and authoritarian. Students alone might be able to reform the university in unimportant ways, but only revolution can transform the university into a dynamic cen-ter for critical thought and action. So even to sustain their hopes as students, they must look outside the university for allies in the struggle for a non-authoritarian socialist society.

At the same time, there are some very immediate, practical reasons for reaching out of academia. The emergency laws have been passed. The public is as hysterically anti-commu-nist (hence anti-anti-authoritarian) as ever. At every demon-stration another student is badly injured or killed—a high price to pay for "revealing the violence" of society. If the movement is going to survive, if movement students are going to survive, they must find allies outside of the university.

At first the SDS students believed that the truth of their ideas was so obvious that, if they could only tear the blinders off people's eyes, adherents would flock to them in masses. In part, they succeeded: direct action did break through the façade of justice and democracy. But no one, except for the students, seemed much disturbed by the ugliness and violence which were so clearly exposed by mass confrontations. Indeed, the press managed to turn direct action tactics against the students and to convince the rest of the population that the students were terrorist criminals. So SDS now believes that the population, however oppressed they may be in Marxist terms, is as effectively integrated as Marcuse said they were. Revolution in Germany is not imminent. New approaches to reaching non-students must be found.

The students, however, have had little experience with conventional organizing. First, they are not sure how to go about building a mass base without compromising their basic positions (who is?). SDS is committed to all-out support for anti-imperialist struggles in the third world, struggles which, at best, seem irrelevant to the average German. SDS opposes authoritarianism in every institution of German society, even when those institutions, like the church or the patriarchal family, may be dear to the hearts of many ordinary people.

Second, the students still see themselves as students. They do not consider dropping out of school to organize. They have only begun to think about what happens to them after they graduate, and, for the most part, still see themselves as following academic careers. The idea of being revolutionary organizers first and foremost, of adapting their way of life to that of the people they are trying to organize, has not yet emerged. For example, there are groups in Berlin doing what American radicals know as community organizing. But unlike the old American SDS Education, Research, and Action Projects (ERAP) and other similar projects, the organizers are not full time organizers; they are still students, and essentially tourists in working class neighborhoods.

Another aspect of the student mentality is the lack of an organizer's time perspective; they are still looking for an immediate response such as they got in the university. They do not think of moving into a community and staying for years. Still another reason they have not been able to break out of the university context is that there is, as of yet, no movement sub-culture (and very little bohemian sub-culture) to sustain non-university radicals. To leave school is, effectively, to leave the movement.

SDS is ambivalent about what to do next. They want to reach out of the university, but they would like to remain students. They need a mass base but they don't want to dilute their stand. Although conditions in West Germany seem critical to SDS, the people are far from revolutionary. The only strategy which seems to them to reconcile these conflicting perspectives is one that we might call "resistance." They argue that in modern Germany, the working class has been pretty well integrated into the capitalist value system, at least for the present. Now, only Germany's marginal group, the students, can even imagine the possibility of alternative forms of society. Their role, then, is to keep alive the idea of a revolutionary alternative: to resist, with all the strength of their imagination, the forces tending to integrate them into passivity, and to keep open the possibility of revolutionary action until others are ready to join the struggle.

Resistance need not be massive to be effective. Decisive minority actions can get a point across. Since the revolutionary group is small compared to the total population, confrontations, leafletings, teach-ins, etc. must take the place of one-to-one organizing. Students can remain students, building their base in the university and sallying out now and then to create a kind of propaganda-by-action. This is an existential strategy, with roots in the unshakeable hopelessness of early SDS: nothing will work, our options are limited, but we must keep trying. As Dutschke wrote, "We lead this conflict with our backs to the wall, without illusory hopes, but we lead it without stopping, and we are convinced of being able to make the anti-authoritarian camp grow by ceaselessly organizing, demonstrating, and educating."

Recently SDS has begun to experiment with more traditional mass organizing as well. If people won't rally to the anti-authoritarian camp, maybe you had better go and find out what's bothering *them*. The issue might be rents and housing, the problems of working mothers, or of high-school students. In Berlin, SDS formed so-called "basis groups" to go out and agitate on non-student problems. One group had worked on housing problems in a working class neighborhood. To us, their expectations seemed inordinately high. For instance, they descended on the neighborhood with the single vague demand of "lower rents." There was none of the careful research characteristic of American community organizing: who really owns the building, what are the laws on maintenance, exactly what repairs are needed? Of course, they did not plan to spend months working through legal tangles and local power structure. In fact, when people failed to immediately connect "lower rents" with more revolutionary challenges to the system, the "basis group" got discouraged. "The women would only talk about housing and rents, but weren't interested in politics," they complained, "and the men weren't interested in the rent. They would only talk about politics." This basis group concluded that rents are not a good radicalizing issue, and after two months, gave up the project. When we told them that American radicals often consider their organizing project a life-long commitment, the SDS'ers looked a little skeptical.

There are also other kinds of organizing attempts just beginning. Some students who have graduated and are now teachers are trying to form a group of radical teachers. Others are working through a social club—the Republican Club— trying to create a base for post-graduate movement activity. But this group, although it served as a coordinating center during some of the events of the spring, is increasingly nothing more than a liberal middle-class social center.

Some of the strongest non-student links to SDS may well come from within the university. At the Free University in Berlin, one particularly liberal institute met and came up with a new constitution which gives a say on all institute matters (including how money is to be spent for research) to everyone who works in the institute—from professors to cleaning ladies. Needless to say, the constitution was rejected by the university administration. As a result of this and other intra-university organizing attempts, about twenty Free University secretaries showed up at an SDS meeting late in the spring of '68. One secretary, who is also an SDS member, told us that secretaries had always known about "authoritarianism" from their relationships with their bosses, but hadn't realized before that SDS had anything to say about such ordinary problems.

The only great non-university successes of the German movement have been with high school students and with apprentices (young workers who learn a skill on the job and go to school part time). The high school students are demanding power, curriculum changes, and easing of sexual repression in the schools. Students in several high schools went out on strike to protest the emergency legislation. The apprentices have been reached both through issues affecting them at work and issues affecting them at school. They have participated in various teach-ins organized by SDS, attended in large numbers the SDS May Day rally in Berlin (attended by 40,000 in all!), and are now forming their own organizations with SDS assistance.

In one town, Bremen (unique in our present context for not having a university), it was the high school students and the apprentices who took the lead in the movement. A small demonstration against an increase in bus fares was brutally broken up by the police. The students and apprentices responded with a rash of demonstrations, sitting down in busy intersections, overturning busses, rioting—completely immobilizing the city for a week. The affair was settled only by negotiations between the elected officials of Bremen and a delegation of sixteen- and seventeen-year-olds. Since these events (in late 1967), these youngsters have developed links to SDS.

The great problems SDS now faces, as it tries to extend its influence beyond the university, are as much internal as external. They tell you that they no longer believe that there is a magic key that will reveal the society to the people and make them rise up in revolt. They talk of the need for the "long march of youth through all the institutions of society." But they have not yet really developed the attitudes for leading a *long* march, through *all* the institutions. Even their much-vaunted theory is geared more for an intellectual student audience than for the exigencies of day-to-day organizing among all sorts of people. These are the problems they must solve, now that they look ahead from having built the most successful mass radical student movement of Europe.

CHAPTER FOUR

Revolt: Italian Style

The Fiat factory is our university.
The university is our Fiat factory.
—Graffito, University of Rome

From Stockholm to Rome, there is not an educational system that escaped charges of repressiveness and authoritarianism in the spring of 1968. Nowhere were the charges more apt than in Italy. All power in the university lies in the hands of the few full professors, who are also the administrators, and frequently also big men *off* campus—in parliament, industry, etc. (For instance, almost every post-war premier of Italy has simultaneously held a university professorship.)

Incoming students face a rigid curriculum, determined as much by tradition as by the professors' tastes. The infrequent exams are oral and help weed out the inarticulate and the troublemakers as well as the unprepared. For the majority of students, yearly exams are the only occasion for coming to the university: scholarships are rare, so only wealthier students have the leisure to actually attend classes. At Turin, 20,000 are enrolled, but only 7,000 attend. The rest work full-time. Classes themselves are hardly attractive, since lectures are usually read by the professor from the text. Discussion is unheard-of and reading primary source material is discouraged. If, for some reason, all the enrolled students decided to attend a class they wouldn't fit in the classroom. For instance, we were told that in the University of Turin, 900 are enrolled in Italian Literature, but the lecture hall has a capacity of 200. Fortunately, no more than 60 ever show up for a lecture.

For an Italian, university life is passive and disengaged, as were high school and grade school. The biggest difference between the university and high school is that in the former, one's interests are purposely narrowed and fragmented. Italian students might endure the suffocation of higher education more cheerfully if there were a reliable pay-off. But most graduates enter the limited job market with what turns out to be obsolete training. For the technical students, industry tries to compensate with on-the-job training. Students in letters, philosophy, architecture, political science, and physics stand the least chance of employment, and often stay in school into their late twenties before settling for whatever job they can find.

Up until the fall of 1967 the national student union (UNURI) was the only organ for student protest. Bureaucratic and top heavy, UNURI attracted little general interest even when it addressed itself to student problems. UNURI factions were linked to adult political parties, and office-holding appealed chiefly to the politically ambitious students. In most universities, elections for UNURI representatives brought out little more than 20 per cent of the vote. When UNURI chapters went so far as to call for strikes and university occupations, students were little more interested than they had been in the elections. After all, UNURI decisions were handed down to the students from above, by people the average student might not even have heard of. Thus, occupations staged by UNURI were so limited and symbolic that today's students do not even consider them "direct action." UNURI failed to mobilize student discontent because it never fathomed the full depth of that discontent, which extended to all forms of bureaucracy and manipulation. When, in 1967, discontent grew into open rebellion, the student union was completely bypassed. (UNURI continues to operate, doing things like running the student travel agency.)

Although Italian students felt directly oppressed *as students,* in Italy, as elsewhere in the Free World, it was Vietnam that was the point of departure for mass student rebellion. Whether Vietnam served initially as a cause, example, or outlet for action on university issues is hard to say. For those students who were already radical, the spectacle of a people armed and struggling for freedom was in jarring contrast to the painstaking maneuvers of the Italian left-wing parties. Vietnam gave them a new sense of urgency and an example of uncompromising militance. Putting this together with the direct-action tactics of black militants in the United States and the confrontation strategy of German SDS, the left students decided that the latent violence of their own society must be met with the open violence of mass struggle.

Not all the students who joined the Vietnam demonstrations in 1966 and 1967 shared the left students' ideological commitment to anti-imperialist struggle. Moral indignation moved the liberals. And probably many other students were propelled by sheer boisterousness, long suppressed by a totalitarian education. Whatever the reasons, Vietnam demonstrations attracted far more students than might have been expected for a country so little involved in the war as Italy. Some students in Turin (where the movement began) trace their involvement to Vietnam meetings and demonstrations in the fall of 1967. At one point, two or three thousand students took to the streets; the police overreacted, and fighting broke out. For many students, it was their first encounter with organized violence. "After that," a student in Turin told us, "I hated the whole system."

* * *

In Turin, the militance lent by Vietnam quickly spilled over into the everyday problems of student existence. Shortly after the violent Vietnam demonstration, the administrative faculty council met to consider a proposal to construct new university faculties outside the city limits. At a meeting of their own, a few hundred students decided they didn't want to be isolated from the city. They delivered a petition to the administrative council and, after the petition was ignored, disrupted the meeting by sitting-in. Police removed the protesting students, but the administration's victory was short-lived. Three days later, on November 27, 800 students occupied the faculties of Letters, Law, Teaching, Political Science, and Philosophy. They made it clear that this occupation was different from the formal, protest-type occupations traditionally undertaken by UNURI: there was nothing to negotiate, because the students had no demands. There could be no demands until all the students had freely discussed the issues. And since normal conditions at the university did not encourage discussion, it was only now, under the occupation, that the discussion could even begin.

The discussion in the liberated buildings quickly ranged far from the narrow issues of student power. "Counter-courses" or liberated seminars dealt with Vietnam, U.S. imperialism in Latin America, teaching methods, philosophy of science, the university in society, psychoanalysis (as a tool to understanding repression), etc. Probably far more important than the content of the counter-courses was the students' discovery that learning could be relevant and exciting. At the end of December the students were ready with their demands: university decisions should be made at general assemblies of the students (by direct, rather than representative, democracy). Groups of students should decide what they want to study and how to go about it. If necessary, a study group would call on an "expert," who might or might not be a professor, for help. There should be no exams and no grades.

The administration responded, predictably, with a bust. Since it was already Christmas vacation, the students were not too reluctant to leave. But for all practical purposes, the University of Turin was not to pick up business-as-usual for the rest of the academic year. As if to prove the point, a crowd of students sneaked back into a police-occupied building through a hole in the wall, then walked out peacefully through the main gate—and through the lines of startled cops. School reopened in January to an almost immediate occupation, this one more massive than the first. "Counter-courses were fun. No one wanted to go back to boring lectures." After the ensuing bust, students decided to stage a "white" occupation (analogous to what Italians call a "white" strike—a slowdown—in industry). They went back into classes and challenged professors from the floor. This tactic—mind-bending for Italians—exposed professorial authoritarianism to many previously apathetic students. The ensuing arrests of unruly students were an even more convincing demonstration of professor-power, and by late January, more than 2,000 students could be counted as active in the movement.

Through the rest of school year, control of the university buildings passed back and forth between the students and the police. Disruption was the rule, but for hundreds of students it was also a year of intense study. People who had previously read only for exams were discovering Marx, Guevara, Mao, and Malcolm X. To student activists throughout Italy, Turin gained a reputation as a center of theoretical work on university issues. Turin was equally influential as a center of activity, and by March student strikes had occurred in high schools and technical schools throughout the region around Turin. In June, the university of Turin reopened after a few minor concessions from the administration. Some activists felt the movement was dead from exhaustion and confusion about goals. (Daily assemblies on perspectives for the movement were drawing "only" about 300 people.) No one, however, expected the university to reopen in the fall with anything less than a massive reoccupation.

The student movement in Rome emerged from a more sharply polarized political setting than that of Turin. On the right, there are semi-organized fascist groupings (the word "fascist" is not used lightly in Italy) composed largely of the sons of Mussolini's civil servants. Left students, ranging from Communist party members to Guevarists, found nothing to agree on outside the Vietnam issue, and little to agree on within it. Although there had been a loose anti-imperialist organization before, the left movement did not really begin until February 1968. A student rally in Florence had been smashed by a brutal police charge onto university grounds. Left students in Rome called a meeting to discuss their response to the events in Florence. Attendance was unexpectedly large, and militant. After lengthy discussion, the students decided to occupy several faculties of the University of Rome.

In retrospect, most activists consider the occupation a failure. First, the occupiers (300 by day and 30 by night) were forced to lock the doors to keep out belligerent fascists. Of course, curious and uncommitted students were locked out with the fascists, without much idea of what the occupiers were up to. Within the occupied buildings, students constituted a general assembly to decide on mass actions, and a series of study groups to propose tactics. The assembly, dominated by the more articulate, already-politicized students, quickly degenerated into a forum for factional disputes. The study groups, where the shyer and less politicized students could get a word in, drifted away from fundamental radical analyses toward reformism. When the police came, at the end of February, the occupiers offered little resistance, escaping through an unguarded gate.

The first occupation of Rome University produced no demands, no organization, no strategy for student power. It did produce the nucleus of what Romans now call "the movement." For a few weeks, a few hundred people had met all day and often all night. Their politics may have ranged from Maoist to university-reformist, but they had all shared the same threat of a police bust or fascist invasion. At the very least, they came out knowing each other and sensing a common enemy.

They did not have to wait long for a test of their new militance. After the bust, the Faculty of Architecture had been closed by the administration, so students decided to use the building for a meeting. During the meeting, scores of cops surrounded the building and demanded that the students come out. The students came out, and were encircled and beaten on the spot. The next day, enraged bystanders, survivors, and sympathizers retaliated by showing up at Valle Giulia park, where no trouble was expected and the guard was light. The onslaught of thousands of angry students took the police completely by surprise. Before reinforcements arrived, several police cars were burned and many people, on both sides, were injured or wounded. (The police encoun-

tered at student demonstrations in Italy are not ordinary
traffic police, but are analogous to New York City's Tactical
Police Force. They are widely hated and feared because of
their strike-breaking activities.) Although 250 students were
taken by the police, Valle Giulia was an outstanding student
victory, inspiring students all over Italy and probably even
in France.

Valle Giulia set the pace for the Roman spring of '68. Two
days after the battle, students reoccupied the Faculties of Letters, Philosophy, Architecture, and Physics. Demands for university reforms were out of the question this time. The occupiers dug into counter-courses on Vietnam, black power, the
Chinese cultural revolution, and the function of the university in Italy. After two weeks, the liberated school ended vio-
lently with an invasion by 150 club-swinging fascists. These
were not fascist students. They were older men, probably
hired thugs. The police stood by and watched for what
seemed like a very long time before joining in the fight. One
student nearly died from club injuries in the back. The
movement that emerged from this second occupation was
larger, bitterly militant, and unquestionably leftist.

The students quickly carried the struggle outside the university. In April, they demonstrated in response to the attempted assassination of Rudi Dutschke. Next, they discovered that the Atomic, Bacteriological, and Chemical Institute
(ABC) was carrying out germ warfare research, on university grounds, for NATO. A sit-in in front of the ABC was disrupted with special enthusiasm by the police, who beat many
bystanders as well as participants. To protest police brutality
and the treatment of arrested students, students held a peaceful demonstration in front of the Palace of Justice, featuring
mock trials of cops and judges. Everything went quietly till
the end, when the demonstrators started for home. Then,

provoked only by the memory of Valle Giulia, the police charged; 190 students were arested and many more were badly beaten.

By May Day the movement was sufficiently confident to march *en masse* to the annual workers' rally. Communist and Socialist trade union bureaucrats were unnerved by the sight of thousands of students, brandishing red flags and sharpened posts (a precaution against the police), mingling easily with the workers. During May, the general elections gave the students a chance for a brief rest: they weren't interested in supporting any party, but didn't want fresh riots to provoke reaction. More important, May brought the near-revolution in France. Dozens of Romans made it to Paris to support the French students at the barricades. Those who stayed behind eagerly discussed every scrap of news from the north.

In early June a demonstration in support of the French students escalated into a riot. Bands of hundreds of students skirmished with police in the narrow streets of a working class section of Rome. In the best French style, barricades were erected and cars were burned, but the local people remained unmoved (except, of course, those who happened to lose a car). Feeling frustrated by the lack of response, the students returned to the university and reoccupied. Their demands, the right to protest and freedom for jailed students, won little sympathy from moderate students preparing for final exams. Fighting between leftist and fascist students led to the year's final occupation—by the police.

Our first, and last, view of Rome University was through heavy lines of riot police. Against the backdrop of blank, functional, Mussolini-era university buildings, they just looked like part of the scenery. Inside, exams were proceeding under the joint proctorship of professors and cops, as if to clarify, to anyone with lingering fantasies of liberal education, just what the movement was all about. The movement continued to "occupy" the men's dorm and made free use of the campus' largest lecture hall for daily general assemblies. We had been warned that the movement was exhausted for the year, that we came too late for the "mass" phase. After four months of nonstop fighting and talking, dozens were in jail and dozens more had gone home for some solid sleep. But every day four or five hundred of the movement met for four or five hours at a stretch, to debate strategy for radicalizing the workers, strategy within the university, theory of revolutionary struggle, etc. There was a sense that, though the fighting was over for a while, the struggle was only beginning.

* * *

No single part of what happened in Italy this spring was entirely unprecedented. Occupations—even fights with fascists and police—were about as much a part of the Italian university scene as beer brawls on American campuses. A student Left, which can trace its genealogy to the World War II resistance fighters, had demonstrated sporadically about Vietnam since 1965. Almost everything that happened in the spring of 1968 had happened before, but this time it happened all over Italy, involving tens, perhaps hundreds of thousands of students, in the space of less than nine months. It was as if the isolated actions of the preceding five years had been compressed into one year and multiplied by the participation of thousands of new people. In 1968, for the first time, neither the issues nor the actions were isolated. Somehow, student-university tensions reached the breaking point at the same time as indignation over the war in Vietnam was hardening into resistance. The issues merged. Disgruntled but apolitical students joined with traditionally left students in a common struggle against authoritarianism —in the university, in the factory, or in Vietnam.

The Italian students had been growing away from the left political parties—Communist (PCI), Socialist (PSI), and Socialist Party of Proletarian Unity (PSIUP)—for several years. No matter how revolutionary their rhetoric or their ancestry, the left parties are bureaucratic and hopelessly addicted to electoral tactics. Many students could justify their party allegiance only in terms of maintaining some connection to the working class, but this became a steadily thinner excuse for party membership. The early sixties were marked by particularly violent strikes, often wildcat, in which it became increasingly clear that the role of the CGIL (the PCI-dominated national confederation of industrial unions) was to dilute the demands of the workers from broad issues, such as workers' control of production, to narrow economic issues like wages and pensions. Student estrangement from the PCI deepened with the development of the third world struggles. While the PCI remained committed to Soviet-style communism, the students were discovering that China, Cuba, and Vietnam, not the USSR, were the standard bearers of world revolution. The PCI lost any remaining credibility in the eyes of left students with its stand on Vietnam, which seemed luke-warm—more a demand for peace than for victory for the National Liberation Front.

To bolster their critique of the "revisionist" PCI, students eagerly studied the Chinese cultural revolution. From Mao they came to understand that revolution is not simply a one-shot affair in which power changes hands, but a continuing struggle against class domination in any form, in any institution. If the revolution was more than a *putsch,* then you didn't have to grow old in the PCI, waiting for that fatal moment when "objective" conditions are ripe and the industrial workers rise up. Revolutionary changes in consciousness could begin at any time, not just at the moment of "the revolution"—so why not now? If students had spearheaded the cultural revolution in China, why couldn't students begin the revolution in Italy? Finally, if the struggle must occur in all institutions, why not start with the university? By this strange circumnavigation—from theoretical concern for the Italian workers to theoretical fascination with the Chinese revolution—the Left students claim to have discovered who and where they were: students at universities. Whether this is a retrospective justification for action on university matters, or a preconceived strategy, doesn't really matter. Radical Italian students, no matter how Left, were feeling the same strains that were producing a mass ground-swell of student rebellion.

For the average student, the tensions generated by the disparity between the Catholic Italy of real life and the consumerist America of the movies have been increasing. This generation of Italian university students is Italy's first fully post-war generation. More than 80 per cent of the students are from middle-class or professional families, and grew up in far greater prosperity than their parents had known. An increasing number of students can afford cars, movies, and summer vacation trips to other European countries. Exposure to less restrictive cultures, especially America's, makes the authority of parents and professors weigh more and more heavily on Italian youth. They are still by no means as well off as American students. Most live at home by necessity, until they get married, which is not until they are able to support a family, which usually means until they are at least thirty. Thus, until they are in their late twenties Italian students live under conditions which would rankle an American thirteen-year-old. Even for older students, dating is uncommon. There is considerable interest in "sexual liberation," but it is still largely confined to theoretical discussions of Wilhelm Reich.

Add to these tensions those induced by a repressive, impersonal, fragmented education, an education which grows increasingly irrelevant to the grown-up business of getting a job. Newly radicalized student activists explained the explosion of 1968 to us very simply: Every year we got more fed up with the university. The only difference between this year and the one before is that, this year, we were more fed up than we were the year before. The majority of today's movement activists were, in October 1967, innocent of left ideology. They came to identify with the third world struggle only through their own struggle, their own problems. They came to read Malcolm, Mao, and Che because they, too, had struggled against authoritarian repression. Like most of the earlier politicized students, the newly radicalized students are completely eclectic. Holistic systems—whether political dogmas or political parties—are rejected as intrinsically authoritarian.

To sum up: In October, 1967, there was a current of anti-imperialism and an ocean of student discontent. Today there is a single movement. The analysis which defines "the movement" is an understanding of the role of the university *vis à vis* the students (unlike the American movement which excels in analyzing the role of the university *vis à vis* other capitalist institutions, such as big corporations). Ideally, the Italians say, the university should teach people to be "critical." That is, it should impart skills, *and* a critical understanding of the use of those skills in the context of the whole society. In fact, the most important skills acquired in the university should be those of questioning, analyzing and criticizing the society and your role in it. But, instead of imparting skills of any kind, the Italian university specializes in instilling the authoritarian ideology of an authoritarian society. "What does the university teach? To command and to obey," we heard again and again. The university takes the undifferentiated mass of students and, through the mechanism of exams, divides them into an elite (the commanders), the future professors and executives, and the upper levels of the working class (the obeyers), the future technicians and white collar workers. Not that the university directly trains people to command: the relation between students and professors is a power relation which the student learns to take either side of. Years of passivity and obedience produce docile workers and dictatorial bosses equally well. By instilling the authoritarian roles of "commander" and "obeyer" and channeling students into one or the other category, the university preserves the class structure of society.

Movement students do not see the authoritarianism of the university as a relic of feudalism, inappropriate to modern industrial society. The authoritarianism of the university is, they believe, inherent in all the institutions of capitalist society. It is capitalism which divides men into producers and owners, workers and bosses, students and professors. In fact, Italian students tend to use the words "capitalism" and "authoritarianism" interchangeably, just as Americans slip between "capitalism" and "imperialism." To attack the university, then, is to challenge the class structure of society—it is to attack capitalism itself, in its "ultimate form."

The attack varies in emphasis from university to university. Roman students believe the university should be challenged only as it functions in reproducing the class system—in examinations. The majority of students cannot afford to attend classes, but everyone, from whatever background, is subject to exams. Since exams are oral, they select for poise and polish, to the detriment of the minority of students from working-class families. Some radicals maintain that even the content of exams favors students from the bourgeoisie. In this context, the Roman activists argue that issues having to do with course content, etc., rather than exams, are bourgeois issues or, at best, distractions.

In Turin, however, the struggle is directed against all manifestations of authority in the university, from exams to one-way lectures. Even the content of education should be challenged, they argue, since it is presented uncritically, for obedient acceptance. The question of how they might deal with reforms, if offered by the administration, has not been considered too carefully in either Rome or Turin. First, meaningful reforms, in the direction of a truly democratic university, would run counter to the interests of the all-powerful professors and the government, and seem to be extremely unlikely. More important, the students feel that the anti-authoritarian thrust of the movement is now so strong that activists will never be satisfied with partial reforms.

By this time the American reader is probably beginning to wonder why we continually refer to Italian student activity simply as "the movement." This is not shorthand for some complex alliance of *groupuscles*. Nor is the movement itself an organization in our sense of the word. It has no name, no membership, no rules, no officers, no program. When an Italian student says he is "in" the movement, he means, roughly, that he participates in demonstrations and assemblies and that his friends do too. Internally, there is no formal structure to the movement. A general meeting in Rome opened with one of the leading activists standing up and asking who would like to chair the meeting. When someone was finally pushed into the chair, he began by asking who would like to talk, and so on. Inevitably a handful of students in Turin and in Rome stood out by virtue of their greater articulateness, intelligence, popularity, or whatever. But no one, least of all themselves, would call them "leaders" or even "spokesmen." Since there are no offices to hold, the only way to function as a leader is to perform well, both in debate and in action. All decisions, whether on strategy or on when to meet next, are made by direct democracy, in the general assemblies.

For all their insistence on direct democracy, the Italians seemed to us to have little notion of participatory democracy. Our first impression of a general assembly was that the students had simply exchanged one set of lectures for another. No speaker ever spoke for less than fifteen minutes, and interruptions from the floor were infrequent. For us, the low point of democracy was at a general meeting in Turin, where one speaker held forth for one hour, while the audience slept, shuffled, whispered, read, or walked in and out. His subject: the failure of the "mass" of the movement to become deeply politicized through intense participation in theoretical discussion! At times of more intense activity or in meetings of less than a hundred, the style, of course, is much looser, with constant give and take.

The form—rather the formlessness—of the movement was just beginning to be discussed when we were in Italy in June. Resistance to any formal structuring runs deep, in the students with political experience as well as their newly radicalized comrades. Many students seem to feel that organizations are authoritarian by their very nature. In any case, they do not see any mechanisms which might ensure democracy and flexibility. From practical experience with UNURI, the PCI, or even PSIUP, they know that organization can harden into bureaucracy, and that bureaucracy can take on a life of its own. For the same reasons they have little interest in developing a comprehensive program or ideology. The spirit is much like that of the first Turinese occupation: The movement is not a struggle for stated goals. The movement is only the context, and the *only* context, in which alternatives can be perceived.

But by June, as the movement was threatening to dissolve into summer vacation, people were beginning to talk about the need for some minimal organization. In Rome there were plans for an office and a newspaper to maintain some sense of unity through the summer. Students who were planning to work with industrial workers felt particularly insecure about the movement's fuzziness, but were still at a loss for organizational forms that could coordinate without dominating. Very likely each university's movement will evolve toward some primitive structure, but something very unlike a party or a union. (In September we heard that students who spent the summer with workers are now developing the beginnings of permanent organizational forms.)

Almost everything we've said about the Italian movement —its anti-authoritarianism, its insistence on direct action and direct democracy—is just about as true for the French, German, or even the American movement. What was unique about the Italian movement was that it seemed (to us, and this reflects a peculiar sensitivity of Americans) blind to all the sociological, psychological, and cultural dimensions of society and social change. It was all muscle and brain. Issues such as developing new life styles or new ways of relating to people, which so preoccupy many Americans, were incomprehensible to the Italians. They had no sense of themselves as a community. When we asked students how people became radicals, the answers were inevitably phrased in moral and intellectual terms, with no mention of "alienation." In fact,

Antonioni notwithstanding, Italian students probably aren't really alienated in the sense we use the term—they are just badly treated.

The movements in Rome and Turin are neither subcultures nor parts of a subculture. No special tastes in music, art or clothing set off the activists from the moderates. By straining, we finally detected slight differences in hair and skirt length between students inside and outside of a movement assembly. There may be a few hippies in Rome, but there was little of what we'd call youth culture. Young people simply cannot afford to live away from home or to express themselves through clothing fads. Movement people usually could not understand why we even bothered to ask whether there were hippies in Italy, where kids went at night for fun, etc.

Nevertheless, the movements in Rome and in Turin certainly seemed to us to have strong elements of community. In some ways they seemed more free-wheeling and less exclusive than many movement communities that have developed in the United States. For instance, in Rome the movement eats dinner in one or another of a few friendly, working-class restaurants. Promptly at nine, everyone piles in, filling the place several times over capacity. At first we thought there were about twenty waiters; then we realized that the students were all helping the single waiter. Generally, only one or two people in the place had any money, and they automatically sponsored the mass meal. Plates were passed back and forth between tables as readily as political observations and jokes about the day's meeting. From this and other scenes, we had no doubt but that the movement is attractive as a community, but the Italians seemed hardly to be aware of it.

This insensitivity to the psychological and sociological aspects of society could, however, become a handicap in dealing with the larger society. For instance, many recognized the growing consumerism of industrial workers, but saw no way of dealing with it. In all fairness, though, we should recognize that it may be years before consumerism outweighs consumption as a working-class problem in Italy. Most students, especially the older ones, were uninterested in attacks on sexual and cultural repression. They dismissed the demonstrations at the Venice Biennale (a biannual art show) as childish, "not really political." Their attitude toward artists was equally uncompromising: "They should do all their work for the movement." No one seemed to have thought much, though, about how art might be used in the service of the movement. As for sex, many students, especially younger ones, would like to make a stab at liberation. A sleep-in was held in the men's dorm at Rome, but it fizzled out. Repression on this issue can be so prompt and effective that many people wonder if it's worth the struggle at this point. For instance a student newspaper in a high school was shut down by the administration just for suggesting that sex education might be a worthwhile subject. In general, attacks on sexual and cultural repression are seen as isolated from the central political themes of the movement. All of the indirect, non-economic means by which society smothers opposition and stifles dissent, from religion to education, are described by the movement as "mystifications." The word "mystification" has become a catch-all for all the repressive sociological and psychological effects that the students cannot analyze, or do not see as analyzable.

* * *

We are writing this in the summer of 1968, when the movement is still less than one year old. The movement, if it keeps moving, should soon be very different from what we have described. It would be futile to try to predict in detail the ways it will go, and grow, in its second year. The Italians themselves see it reaching increasingly outside the university gates. They have no illusions about reforming the university. With the Germans and the French, they believe that there can be no democratic university in an undemocratic society. Students alone cannot transform the society; they must make alliances with people of other classes and other occupations. To the more politically experienced students, blue-collar workers are the key to change. Italian workers are relatively class-conscious and militant compared to American workers, but there are enormous barriers between them and the students. First, the class difference and concomitant difference in life-style make students feel that going to live in working class areas would be a foolish gesture. Students are also hesitant to take jobs in factories, since jobs are scarce and any influx of new workers might be resented by the old.

But the steepest barrier between students and workers is the Communist-dominated trade union confederation, the CGIL. The CGIL cannot be simply bypassed in dealing with the workers, since it is their union, and it is credited by the workers with most of their economic gains. Students feel that, in their organizing, they must somehow respect the CGIL as a protective working class organization, while attacking it as a bureaucracy. For instance, they will try to organize presently unorganized workers (into CGIL or independent unions) but not without simultaneously implanting a firm resistance to authority and bureaucracy. One approach which some students favor is the easy-going style of early (American) SNCC, which aimed at developing local initiative and leadership. One tactic is to support a strike, with pickets and demonstrations, and use the opportunity to discuss the nature of the demands with the workers. The students try to encourage the workers to express their militance rather than submit to the cautious trade union bureaucracy. While we were in Rome, movement students were participating in a strike by the janitors and cooks of the men's dorm. The workers were enthusiastic about the students' moral and material support, but still dubious about raising demands for "self-management," or control of decision-making on work issues.

All over Italy student-worker relations are still confined to a measure of mutual respect and a few contacts, but CGIL leaders are already showing signs of nervousness, or at least ambivalence. Within the PCI, "student contacts" are a source of some status, yet the PCI condemned the spring student demonstrations as "adventurist." The PCI and the CGIL feel that students should stick to university issues.

Yet another obstacle to an effective student-worker alliance may be the relative green-ness of the student movement itself. If the more experienced students are cautious about organizing workers, the great majority of newly radicalized are baffled. They have only recently discovered that it's possible to resist oppression in their own lives—let alone someone else's, in which the issues and the style may be totally unfamiliar. In Turin, student "leaders" made the mistake of rushing into the spring Fiat strike without much explanation to their classmates. They returned to the university to find the movement confused and demoralized.

However, there are reasons to think that the barriers to a student-worker movement in Italy are not insurmountable. First, Italian workers continue to have serious unresolved grievances over wages and working conditions, and it seems unlikely that any long period of industrial peace is at hand. Second, the movement insists on mass interactions between students and workers, not just contacts between representatives of students and representatives of workers. This makes the students harder for the CGIL to handle. At the same time, it restrains "inspired" minorities from dashing off to the workers with nothing to offer but advice.

We can hardly expect a movement as young as Italy's to display finesse in dealing with established trade unions or the cultural hegemony of capitalism. Italian students have absorbed Mao, but not Marcuse. They have fought with cops, but not with liberals. And movement students will be the first to tell you so. So far the movement has been characterized by a straightforward rejection of adult authoritarian institutions—universities, political parties, etc. The movement has proved its genius for fighting cops and "demystifying" classrooms and courtrooms. Now most students feel that greater subtlety will be required for "the long march" through the other institutions. They need an analysis to equip them for the confrontation with left-wing parties, with Parliament and with other integrative institutions. Above all, they need a critique and a vision which can be shared with workers as well as students.

CHAPTER FIVE

France: The Short Spring

The question of whether revolution is still possible in the advanced capitalist countries doesn't interest me.
—Daniel Cohn-Bendit

Je suis Marxiste, tendance Groucho.
—Graffito, Paris, June 1968

The high point of the student movements of all the countries of Europe in the spring of 1968 was, of course, May in France. The student movement in France had mushroomed in the spring of 1968, leading to violent clashes with the police. In sympathy, the national confederations of trade unions called a one-day general strike and a giant demonstration. But the workers had grievances, too, and once their energies were unleashed, they could not be imprisoned. Factory after factory was occupied by its workers, until, by late May, ten million workers were on strike. Tens of thousands of students and workers marched through Paris, demanding "workers' power, peasants' power, and students' power," waving red flags, and singing the *Internationale*. The revolutionary wave swept over people in provincial towns too. At Nantes, the entire town was run as a commune by the workers.

The threat of revolution had come out of the jungles of Southeast Asia and down from the highlands of Latin America. For the first time in decades, an advanced capitalist state tottered on the edge.

The student movement which touched off the tumultuous events of May was a young movement. There is no organization whose history we can trace, as we can trace the story of German SDS, through slow preparatory years. Nevertheless, the roots of the French student revolt are much the same as in other European countries. As elsewhere, Vietnam and the crisis of the educational system were the initial causes for agitation. The difference between France and the other European countries is that in France the working class was becoming more militant on its own, so that when the students lit the spark, the workers' movement caught fire. This, in turn, entirely transformed the student movement. Instead of following a course like other young student movements which were born in the fall of 1967 (such as the Italian movement), it leaped far beyond the confines of the university, and completely changed our perceptions of the nature, role, and possibilities of students as revolutionaries.

An intensely politicized student population is nothing new to France. During the Algerian War, thousands of French students risked their careers and sometimes their lives to oppose French imperialism. With the end of the war and the rise of de Gaulle, activity waned, and most students went back to their books. De Gaulle's immense popularity seemed to leave no opening for attack. Besides, domestic issues were much more subtle than an imperialist war. It wasn't until 1965-66 that students found a clear focus for political activity again: the American war in Vietnam. A shadow of the urgency of the Algerian years returned, and many hundreds again became active. For the first time in years there was an issue which could rally apolitical and liberal students, as well as the ideologically committed. In a sense, Vietnam was an easy evasion of domestic issues. Even de Gaulle was against the war. But at the same time, Vietnam provided a hot-house atmosphere for budding militants. In opposing the war, you could talk and even act militantly without ever confronting the power of the state or of established Left organizations such as the giant Communist Party.

What turned this militance into a mass movement, however, was the growing crisis in the universities. As in other European countries, university enrollment accelerated wildly in the 1960's. From 1960 to 1964 alone, the number of students attending the university grew by sixty per cent. Then from 1965-68, the post-war baby boom added to this mushrooming student body. At the same time, the patterns of use of the university were shifting to meet the changing industrial demands. Enrollment in the Medical and Law Faculties dropped, relatively, as students shifted into the Faculties of Letters and of Sciences. The experience of attending the overcrowded universities became ever more alienating. As in Italy, professors read from their own textbooks to gigantic lecture classes. And large though the classes seemed, they contained only the small fraction of enrolled students who could fit into the classroom. The rest didn't even try; they bought a copy of the professor's lectures and read them at home.

Faced with a university which was meeting neither the needs of business for highly educated workers nor the needs of the students for a decent education, the government, like governments throughout Europe, had to initiate reforms of some kind. All of the reforms aimed at making the educational process speedier and more efficient. Up to now, everyone who passed his baccalaureate exam at the end of high school was automatically admitted to the university. Once in, many students dragged out their stay almost indefinitely by working part-time. One of the planned reforms would superimpose further selection procedures on the "bac" and then eliminate part-time study for the lucky entrants. The curriculum reforms, proposed in 1963 by Fouchet, then Minister of Education, would channel entering students into one of several specialized paths: one would lead to academic research, another to narrow, non-theoretical training as a technician, another to teaching. Training in liberal arts and training in sciences would be neatly separated—if possible, in separate buildings.

Thus, the old wholesale wine market in Paris was demolished to make way for the new Faculty of Science, at a safe distance from the Faculties of Letters and Philosophy. Far out on the outskirts of Paris, near a train station appropriately named La Folie ("madness"), a new Faculty of Letters rose from the fields of Nanterre. But new buildings cannot up-date curriculum and teaching methods. The transplanted students found they had the same old grievances, plus the added problem of geographical isolation. Nanterre is situated in what can only be described as a very large field of mud.

If the old university had been oppressive, the "reformed" one would be intolerable. One of the early complaints about the Fouchet Plan was not, however, its content, but that students had never been consulted in drafting it. From this first notion of their own right to make "the decisions that affect their lives," the next question was obvious for the students: who *did* make the decisions? The Ministry of Education, the national government. And from there, why did they make *this* decision? In the interests of business and government, certainly not for the students' sake. Then the final question was: why should our education, in fact our careers, serve *them,* anyway? Students asked the same questions all over France. At Nanterre and at the Sorbonne, at Strasbourg and at Nantes, student protest movements sprang up in the spring and fall of 1967.

In France, discontent escalated very rapidly to articulate protest. For one thing, the French educational system, like almost everything else French, is highly centralized. It is the Minister of Education, not the professors or the rector of a university, who has the power to initiate reforms. When agitation erupted into action, local authorities were powerless to meet it with even minor adjustments. The whole affair got dumped on the steps of the Ministry of Education. For the students, conflict with the university meant conflict with the state.

At this point, many of the students were on familiar ground. Marxism is ingrained in French student culture much the way liberalism is a part of American student culture. This sort of "cultural Marxism" may not have affected the way many students acted before 1967 or 1968, but it certainly determined the way they thought about their situation. Revolution, class struggle, socialism, a mystique of the working class—the ideas were all there long before they took living form in May.

* * *

In the fall of 1967, the agitation over the war in Vietnam and over the growing university crisis converged. The Fouchet Plan was put into full operation just as the universities were swept by the largest wave yet of incoming students. Student political interest revived. There was not yet, however, anything one could pinpoint as "the movement." The only left-wing organizations on the scene were the *groupuscules*. These tiny groups, each with its own sectarian analysis of the "correct" tasks for the Left, competed for student support. A few students joined one or another—especially the Trotskyist *Jeunesse Communiste Révolutionnaire* (JCR) and *Fédération des Étudiants Révolutionnaires* (FER) and the Maoist *Union de la Jeunesse Communiste* (*Marxiste-Léniniste*). Others passed through them, first looking for quick answers, then becoming more and more turned off by the sectarianism and sterility of these groups, and finally quitting. Most students, however left they considered themselves in principle, never bothered with the *groupuscules*.

The initial lead in the events which led to May was taken not by the *groupuscules* of the Left, but by the national union of students (the *Union Nationale des Étudiants de France*, UNEF). In the first semester of the 1967-68 school year, the UNEF called for a week of protest activities around the crisis in the universities. Included was a brief student strike. At Nanterre, more than ten thousand students participated in the strike and won a few modest reforms. Most notably, joint student-faculty "committees of peers" were set up to discuss how to improve the university. But even this "victory" was short lived. The students soon discovered that the student-faculty committees had no power and were in little danger of even being listened to.

When it seemed that the UNEF wasn't going to accomplish much more, leadership passed over to less orthodox people. At Nanterre, especially, it was a small group of *les enragés* along with a number of *groupuscule* students who took the lead. All through the fall and winter, these people had been agitating the students and provoking the administration. They instigated a "sleep-in" in the women's dormitory to demand that men be permitted to visit women in their rooms. From the Germans they picked up the "go-in": they would enter a classroom and demand an immediate debate with the lecturer. Or they would occupy the lecture room next door to a regular class and deliver a counter-lecture or hold a critical discussion of the professor's lectures. The leftists also called for a boycott of the spring "partial" examinations. Exams, they argued, were the mainstay of the university's oppression and manipulation of the student. Exams give students their number, their price tag for the outside world. Exams force students to regurgitate the ideological nonsense their professors have pumped into them. With exams, they said, the university undertakes its primary act of violence against the autonomy of the students' existence. At Nanterre, many hundreds risked failing, in order to observe the boycott.

Meanwhile, the heat from Vietnam was beginning to be felt within the university as well as on the streets of Paris. Anti-war sentiment ran high, and in March 1968 offices of several American companies in Paris were hit by plastic explosives. The American Embassy became the target of stone-throwing demonstrators. As a result, six students were arrested, including two from Nanterre. On March 22, leftist students at Nanterre held a meeting to protest the arrests of their comrades. The *enragés* argued that an appropriate protest need not be directed against the police, who had performed the arrests. Arrests were the act of the whole system, of which the police were merely the armed wing. Therefore it was appropriate to respond by attacking the system in any of its institutions. Since they were in a university, one of the key institutions of the system, it was the university they should attack. And so 142 students, *groupuscule* and independent, occupied the administration building. They talked through the night, and decided to continue their movement, calling it after the day of the protest, the *Mouvement du 22*

Mars (the March 22nd Movement). As their next act, they planned a meeting to take place one week later—a giant discussion session.

The following week was a turbulent one at Nanterre. Students handed out leaflets and invaded classrooms to advertise the meeting. A far-right-wing group of students, *Occident* (whose mentors, revanchist paratroopers from the Algerian War, had taught them such political skills as hand-to-hand combat), threatened to disrupt the meeting. The rector of the university panicked. Late in the afternoon of the day preceding the meeting, he ordered the university closed for the next day and for the weekend immediately following, and attacked the "group of irresponsible students who for several months have disturbed classes and examinations." Minister of Education Peyrefitte predicted the decline of the movement: the *enragés,* he said, are "discrediting themselves more and more in the eyes of the mass of students. . . ." The students were not scared off; they rescheduled the meeting for April 2.

Nothing builds a movement so rapidly as repression. On April 2, the 142 students who had formed the March 22nd Movement found that they had brought out 1,200 students to the meeting. They took over a large amphitheater and began to talk. First they mapped out a program of educational and ideological work for the remainder of the academic year, featuring two "anti-imperialist" days. Then the students broke up into discussion groups, with orders to keep talking until a position had been worked out. There were sessions on Anti-Imperialist Struggles, on Culture and Creativity, on Critique of the University and the Critical University, on Eastern Europe, on Student Struggles and Worker Struggles, on Examinations, and many other subjects.

But events were to prove that "educational and ideological

work" was not enough. The struggle escalated rapidly. On April 3 a government committee announced that beginning in 1969, admissions to the university would no longer be un-limited. On April 19, following the attempted assassination of the German student leader Rudi Dutschke, two thousand students rallied in the Latin Quarter to demonstrate their solidarity with German SDS. Two days later, an extraordi-nary convention of the UNEF to elect a new president was disrupted and finally destroyed by rightists. On April 22, five thousand students demonstrated peacefully in solidarity with the Vietnamese people. On April 27, Dany Cohn-Bendit, one of the most prominent of the *enragés* at Nanterre, was ar-rested and questioned at length by the police. The next day, the right-wing *Occident* threatened to "crush the Bolshevik vermin."

As a result of these events, the first of the planned anti-imperialist days, May 2, found the students restless and tensed for possible violence between right and left. The rector at Nanterre decided once more to forestall trouble by closing the university, thus locking out the "anti-imperialists." The stu-dents, unable to meet in their own university, went to the Sorbonne in Paris to tell people what had happened.

On Friday, May 3, students gathered in the courtyard of the Sorbonne. Soon they found they were surrounded by policemen who claimed to be "protecting" them and refused to let anyone leave the courtyard. As it turned out, the cops were there under orders from Sorbonne Rector Roche to clear the whole faculty of students. Late that afternoon the police moved in and arrested almost six hundred students, with un-called-for brutality. The following Monday the students marched through the Latin Quarter, demanding the libera-tion of the arrested students. Twenty thousand strong, they chanted, "We are a *groupuscule*, a dozen *enragés*." In the evening, the police moved in again, and in the battle that followed, four hundred more were arrested, and a total of six hundred policemen, students, and bystanders were injured.

Students' anger continued to mount. The next day a crowd estimated variously as thirty to sixty thousand marched. The UNEF and the union of university teachers called for a strike, demanding amnesty for those arrested, reopening of the faculties, and the withdrawal of the police from the Latin Quarter as a precondition to negotiations. But the government would not give, and by May 10, the students were determined to recapture the Latin Quarter. The government played its part, and ordered the riot police to clear the streets.

May 10, 1968, the "night of the barricades." Helmeted students overturned hundreds of cars and trucks. Gas tanks were emptied to fill Molotov cocktails and the vehicles pushed into the streets as barricades. When the police charged, the students ignited the flimsy outer barricades and retreated behind a second, sturdier line. The police bombarded the students with tear gas grenades and concussion grenades and the students retaliated with cobblestones. "I never felt the gas," a veteran told us later, "I was never more alive." Occupants of the buildings lining the narrow streets threw down cold water and wet cloths for the gassed students. The police, perhaps rightly, considered everyone in the quarter their enemy. They beat anyone they could find in the streets, as well as any they could drag out of their apartments into the streets. The toll was 460 arrested, 367 injured, and unverified accounts of several dead in what had been the fiercest street-fighting since the Liberation of Paris in 1944. When we were in Paris four weeks later, the Latin Quarter looked like a newly occupied colony: boarded-up store fronts, gutted cafes, and pitted streets, all well patrolled by squads of police armed with submachine guns.

Government violence had gone too far this time. Thousands of ordinary citizens had watched students being beaten systematically with clubs and rifle butts, dragged through the streets by their hair, kicked to unconsciousness, or drenched with liquid tear gas. The government hastily tried to retreat before the enraged populace. Faculties would be reopened, and the police withdrawn from the Latin Quarter. Premier Pompidou promised that the cases of the arrested students would be reconsidered. But it was too late to make amends. As the police withdrew, students rushed back in and re-took the streets. As the faculties opened, students moved in and occupied them. As arrested students and workers were released, they rejoined their comrades in the Latin Quarter. Then came the nearly irreversible step towards revolution: the biggest national confederations of trade unions, the Communist-controlled CGT (*Confédération Générale du Travail*) and the independent CFDT (*Confédération Française Démocratique du Travail*) called for a one-day general strike. Monday, May 13, was set aside to protest police brutality and to raise the workers' own demands for higher wages, shorter hours, and union rights.

Monday came, and something like a million people demonstrated, marching through the streets of Paris. What had begun on May 2 as a student anti-imperialist day had become on May 13 a vast anti-government demonstration. At the end of the massive procession, despite the opposition of the trade union leadership, the March 22nd Movement called for a collective discussion of the day's events and of the tasks ahead. Many workers obeyed the union leaders and went home, but thousands of others marched to the Eiffel Tower to join the students. On the Champ de Mars at the base of the tower, the two crowds mingled and talked well into the night .

Tuesday evening brought electrifying news. The Sud-Aviation plant, near Nantes, was not going back to work. The workers had seized their factory. From Nantes the occupation movement spread like wildfire. The next day, while the students were occupying the Odéon Theater for use as a vast public debating hall, workers at the Renault factories, first at Cléon and then at Flins, occupied their factories. Factory after factory, studios, labs, train stations, work places of every kind were occupied by their workers. Even fourteen-year-old children occupied their schools. By the beginning of the following week, the country was paralyzed. Ten million workers, two-thirds of the entire work force, were on strike. The demands in some quarters escalated from higher wages to "workers', peasants', and students' power," and *autogestion* (workers' self-management).

France teetered on the edge of full-scale revolution. Everywhere people met—in cafes, ex-theaters, ex-schools, factories, streets—the topics of discussion were the same: grievances against de Gaulle; *autogestion;* self-defense of occupied factories; have we gone too far? have we gone far enough? Every day brought new rumors: that de Gaulle was massing troops in Alsace, that the police were ready to join the strike, that the government buildings in Paris would be captured by the workers. At Cannes some of France's leading film directors disrupted the film festival. In Paris, students and workers clashed almost daily with the police. In the countryside, peasants carted their produce to the workers in occupied factories. Throughout it all, the harried bureaucrats of the CGT haggled night and day for wage increases and better working conditions. After many days they brought a "settlement" back to the workers only to be hooted down, and sent back, sheepishly, for more. Neither party to the negotiations, the trade unions nor the government, seemed to know what to do. One rumor had it that senior government officials were bundling up their papers and preparing to flee. On the international markets, the mighty franc trembled in the winds of revolution.

In the last week of May, de Gaulle finally made his stand. If the government was going to change, he was going to be the one to change it. He dissolved the National Assembly and called for new elections. The mood of the people shifted rapidly. Many solid citizens, shopkeepers, white collar workers, etc. began to feel that the holiday was over. Revolution is fun for a while, but if you can't count on the electricity and the corner bar is running out of cigarettes, well, maybe things have gone too far. Besides, de Gaulle might have a point about the danger of "totalitarian Communism."

Actually, as de Gaulle must have realized, the Communist Party was the least of his worries. All along, the CGT and the Communist Party had done their best to cool things, knowing full well that they would fall in the face of the workers' demands for power before the government did. So when de Gaulle called for elections, the Party cheerfully repressed all memory of Lenin and decided to continue the struggle in electoral politics, not in the factories and streets. They pressured the workers, sometimes ruthlessly, to go back to work and forget about *autogestion*. They condemned students and militant workers as "adventurists" or "provocateurs." In case that wasn't enough to keep students away, CGT goons were posted at the factory gates of some factories near Paris. Thousands of workers, appeased by wage increases or demoralized by the collapse of their leadership, began to filter back to work. Thousands of very unrevolutionary people, caught up in the forward thrust of May, came to their normal senses

ed they didn't want a revolution. Thousands of
frightened by the violence and chaos of May, de-
vote for de Gaulle, their only bastion against anarchy. The threat of revolution faded into anecdotes, and, in
late June, the Gaullists won a landslide victory.

The last holdouts were the students. They weren't driven
out of their occupied buildings by any misgivings about the
revolution, but by the police. When the tide went out in
June, a revolutionary contingent was left. There were thousands of students who could never again sit through a lecture, thousands of students who could never fit themselves
into the narrow limits of a profession. Whatever they had
been in April was forgotten in June. Again and again in conversations we heard the sentence, "Before May I was a chem-
ist," or "an existentialist," or "a kid." What happened before
May, the events and issues leading up to the barricades, could
have been a whole chapter in the story of another country's
student movement. To the French students, all that was
preface. It was important because it led to May, but everything that follows, follows from May.

* * *

To understand the organizations and the people who
emerged from May as revolutionary, you have to try to understand how haphazard the whole thing was. There was no
cell of revolutionaries, no party organization, propelling
events to a final confrontation. The workers vacillated between loyalty to the Communist Party and the gambler's im-
pulse to keep pushing for a win. The Party scrambled to keep
a millimeter ahead of the workers, without seeming too forward to the government.

The students were not, in any traditional sense, organized

at all. Their "organization" was the March 22nd Movement, which spread from Nanterre faster and farther than its adherents could have traveled. In fact, March 22nd wasn't an organization at all; it was a name, a rallying cry, a style, a way of acting. If you were active and you liked what you had heard of March 22nd, then you were "in" March 22nd. It was at any time the sum of the people who were acting and the embodiment of their ideas. If March 22nd has to be classified as an organization, then we would call it multi-tendency in ideology and anarchistic in form. It could hardly have been otherwise, since it did not grow by recruitment, but by accretion of new groups and new individuals as they moved into action. The test of March 22nd's "organizational" strength came in June, when the government ordered it, along with several other groups, to dissolve. Since there were no officers, no members, and no membership cards, the dissolution order had no effect on March 22nd activities. (As we shall see, it was the decline of the action period of May and June that eventually led to March 22nd's decline.)

The local mode of action during May and June also emerged in the course of the struggle. After May 13, *Comités d'Action* (Action Committees) sprang up in universities and schools, in factories and in neighborhoods. Groups of foreigners such as Algerian, Portuguese, Spanish, and Italian workers, and even Americans, started *Comités d'Action*. By early June, there were three or four hundred active action committees, mainly in the Paris area. Each committee undertook the tasks that seemed appropriate to its constituency and its abilities. Thus, an occupied faculty at the university would have committees for propaganda, posters, internal education, cooperation with workers, and sometimes even an overall committee coordinating the others. A neighborhood in Paris would have action committees raising money,

putting up posters, distributing leaflets, organizing people
for demonstrations, or selling movement newspapers. The
action committees were coordinated only loosely and sporadically. They would meet and discuss possible common actions,
the overall orientation of the action committees, the tasks to
be done. Specific directives were not handed down to individual committees. Instead, each group took on the responsibility of doing what it felt it could handle.

The principle that kept all these diverse groups together
was "unity on action, diversity on ideology." There was no attempt to hammer out a common program or detailed set of
demands. For example, most of the action committees opposed de Gaulle's special June elections and condemned the
Communist Party's participation as "reformist." But the
grounds for opposition varied from committee to committee
and from neighborhood to neighborhood. Some argued
that elections were a diversion, a way of dividing the workers
and diverting attention away from the real problems. Others
argued that elections were not democratic because young
people, eighteen to twenty-one, who had played such a prominent role thus far, could not vote. Others pointed out that
the election laws were rigged so that the left parties ended
up with fewer representatives in Parliament than their
strength among the electorate warranted. Others argued
that elections were irrelevant in any case, that representational forms, however egalitarian, are really anti-democratic,
that only direct participation without intermediaries was
really democratic. In short, the opposition to participation in
the elections ranged from broad ideological rejection of
electoral action as a revolutionary tactic to narrow tactical
opposition to *this* election. But this diversity did not prevent
the action committees from working together for a boycott
of the elections. The action committees shared an anti-gov-

ernment, anti-capitalist ideology; they could cooperate in working against the government and against capitalism. That was all, but in May, it seemed to be enough.

The ideological diversity of the March 22nd Movement derived in part from the diverse groupuscular backgrounds of many of the activists. Not everyone was changed by the events of May to the same degree or even in the same direction. One group in particular, the *Jeunesse Communiste Révolutionnaire* (JCR), managed to resist total submergence in the March 22nd Movement and to keep its line consistent throughout the May chaos. Begun in 1965 as a Communist youth group spin-off, JCR became the standard bearer for traditional Marxism-Leninism within March 22. JCR owed its durability to its flexibility in action (few other *groupuscules* even saw fit to fight at the barricades) and its ideological eclecticism. From Trotsky they picked up the idea of permanent revolution, and from Guevara the idea of multiple revolutions. Che's phrases—"two, three, many Vietnams" and "the duty of a revolutionary is to make a revolution"— practically served as punctuation in our conversations with JCR people. They saw imperialism as the key issue for revolutionaries in advanced countries, though by "imperialism" they often seemed to mean "capitalism." Organizationally they adhered to the traditional "democratic centralism" of the orthodox Communist and Trotskyist parties.

JCR accommodated itself to the events of May, but it did not change in any fundamental way. As the movement waned in June, they were the first to revert to a pre-May kind of defeatism. Foreseeing a prolonged period of police repression and covert struggle, they decided that what the movement needed was a party to hold it together. So, from above, without prior discussion with the mass of activists, JCR joined with some Communists (who had left the Party because of its behavior in May) to announce the formation of the *Mouve-ment Révolutionnaire,* the new party which was to replace the Communist Party. The new party would be democratic-centralist in structure and highly disciplined. Nothing could have been farther from the minds of most of March 22nd.

Even from JCR the proposal seemed out of character, since they had persistently attacked the Communist Party as hierarchical and bureaucratic. We asked one JCR member how he expected the new party to escape the fate of the old. His only answer was to quote Lenin to the effect that the party's devotion to militancy and to revolutionary action would keep it alive and democratic even though it was highly centralized and disciplined. This seemed to be a pretty feeble answer since the party Lenin had spoken of, in its French incarnation at least, is neither democratic nor militant any more. Needless to say, the *Mouvement Révolutionnaire* aroused massive apathy in the non-JCR majority of the March 22nd Movement. It remains in name only, on scattered leaflets and probably in the copious files of the Paris police.

Ironically, the very tightness of organization which the JCR extolled made the JCR itself extremely vulnerable to police repression. Since June, many leaders have been picked off and arrested, and pathways of communication within JCR have been severely disrupted.

JCR has received an undue amount of attention. It is even considered by some people to have been the leading group in the May events. We think this is something of an optical illusion. JCR's tightness of organization and ideological homogeneity made it easily recognizable at all stages in the struggle. Historians of an orderly frame of mind will undoubtedly single out JCR from the confused anarchy of May. Furthermore, JCR conforms to the popular image of a revolutionary party—an image which ordinary newspaper readers share with many older leftists.

Even before the abortive *Mouvement Révolutionnaire* proposal, JCR was well out of the mainstream of the March 22nd Movement, both in ideology and in style. The mainstream of March 22nd was Marxist in analysis, militant in style, and anti-authoritarian at heart. Up to a point, most March 22nd activists could have found much to agree with even in the thinking of the Communist Party: Capitalism is the root of all evils, from imperialism to no-cal foods. The state is the instrument of the ruling class of capitalists. Both will be overthrown in class struggle led by the industrial workers.

There the agreement would end. March 22nd rejected the authoritarianism, the bureaucracy, and the lack of spontaneity of the Communist Party, just as they rejected the authoritarianism, bureaucracy, and lack of spontaneity of French capitalist society. In its ideals March 22nd was anti-authoritarian; in its idea of revolutionary action it was anti-authoritarian; in its actions it was anti-authoritarian.

March 22nd never really had a strategy or saw the need for one. They did have a tactic: direct action. Multiplied many times over it becomes, we guess, a strategy itself. March 22nd students did not see themselves as "leaders," as an "avant garde" who go out and carefully organize to "raise the consciousness" of the workers. Instead, they saw themselves as having been the "active minority" which "plays the part of a permanent fermenting agent, encouraging action without claiming to lead. . . . It is spontaneity which permits the thrust forward, and not the slogans or directives of a leading group." (Cohn-Bendit) In May, this ferment began in the university, among students, but this need not always be true. Next time inspiration could strike some other group.

The mechanisms of "fermenting" are confrontation and "exemplary action." You act on a set of issues, a situation. By acting you provoke a confrontation which exposes the real nature of the situation and forces people to take sides. For instance, confronting university officials on a university issue may lead to their responding by calling the police. This exposes the way in which the university is dependent on the power of the state, and reveals the latent violence and authoritarianism in the day-to-day social relations which most people normally accept.

Another, perhaps more trivial, example comes from the early May days at Nanterre: meetings of students and of professors were held simultaneously but separately in adjoining auditoriums. The professors hesitantly proposed that the students send in a representative to explain to them what they were thinking and doing. To the students, this request smacked of professorial aloofness and authoritarianism. The chairman of the student session yanked open the door between the two auditoriums and angrily told the professors that if they wanted to talk and to cooperate in any way with the students, they must immediately come in and meet with them as equals, *en masse*. If they weren't willing to do that, they should forget the whole thing—go back to their academic studies and forget that anything was happening. "Take it or leave it." The professors, somewhat shamefacedly, took it—they came in and joined with the students. Once people have been forced to choose, to take sides, then according to March 22nd, you can begin to talk to them more reasonably.

To March 22nd, direct action was not just a lively new style of protest. The pattern of direct action was not seen as a reaction to events, but as the *creation* of events. Thus, the importance of acting went beyond the narrow aims of any particular action. For action shows people that they can take their fate into their own hands. Action shakes people loose from old habits of inertia and transforms them from objects of history to agents of history. There is no such thing, the activists insisted, as "being" anti-capitalist or "being" revolutionary. Revolutionary militance is not a state of grace or a salaried position in the Communist Party; it is a way of acting. What is more, it is a way of acting *now*. You don't have to sit around and wait for the appropriate "objective conditions" anymore than you have to wait for a call from the Central Committee. "Objective conditions" for revolution are something to create, not something to wait for. In these terms, the students didn't see themselves as leading the workers at any time, only as setting an example. As Cohn-Bendit said, "The active minority was able . . . to light the first fuse. . . . But that's all. The others could follow or not follow. It happens that they followed."

The value of "exemplary action" seemed to be confirmed in May. Students acted, setting the example, and the workers proceeded to act on their own. But as the movement began to collapse in June, some students had time to reflect back on pre-May history. They pointed out that the isolated cases of direct action in the months and years before May 1968 hadn't caught on outside the university at all, much less snowballed into near-revolution. And in June all the attempts to re-stimulate the lagging workers' struggle were failing. The workers were slowly, inexorably, dropping out of the battle. Maybe there *was* something special about May 1968, even "objectively" special. They began to accept the idea that mass struggle can only be created on some sort of sub-stratum of objective conditions. In between the moments of apocalyptic mass action, there would have to be intervals of minor confrontations and sustained organizing.

In any movement other than March 22nd, the prospect of a long period of relative inaction would probably drive activists into theoretical work—analysis of objective conditions, the temper of the working class, the role of students, etc. In March 22nd, attitudes toward "theory" range from outright rejection to a mild pragmatic interest. The more anarchist students believe that theorizing is a form of evasion. They believe that the kind of strategic thinking left groups traditionally engage in is fundamentally misguided, because it assumes that society is static enough to analyze. Actually, they say, there is nothing constant enough to theorize about. Action changes people, changes situations, and changes people's view of situations. "How can I tell you what I will do months from now?" a March 22nd activist asked us. "I am a different person than I was months ago. I can tell you about tomorrow; I can guess about Sunday; but I cannot imagine 'a few months from now'; I will be a different person then."

So long-range thinking becomes impossible. There is neither a stable substratum to think about nor a stable thinker to do the thinking. Not all the activists are so sophisticated, however, in their distrust of theory. After years of rhetoric from the Communists and the *groupuscules,* they've just had enough talk. We asked one student whether he had been influenced by reading certain revolutionary theoreticians. He thought for a minute and decided not: "It doesn't matter to me what people say, only what they do."

Other students are not such hard-line anti-theorists. Now that the action which broke out almost spontaneously in May has died down, they recognize the value of long-range planning and thinking. But their theoretical concerns are in many ways very different from those of the student movement in the United States.

Many American New Left theorists believe that the American system is a new stage of capitalism, unforeseen by Marx, in which the bitterness of the class struggle has been reduced by the integration of the working class into the value system of their exploiters, the capitalists. The French students believe that they are operating in a more old-fashioned, brutal form of capitalism. As long as the working class is poor and oppressed by heavy-handed employers and a heavy-handed government, there is little danger that it will be peacefully "integrated."

In the U.S., much New Left theory has been concerned with distinguishing between reformist demands, which only integrate the workers more deeply into the system, and revolutionary demands, which could unhinge the workers from the system. To the French, such distinctions are meaningless. Given the predictably crude responses of the government, *any* demand will provoke sharp struggles which can lead to revolutionary consciousness and revolutionary action. The question is how to develop struggle around such demands in such a way that masses of workers, not just a handful of their "representatives," become involved. In other words, how do you get past the trade unions? Workers rely on their union for protection, no matter how bureaucratic or corrupt that union is. How, then, do you get workers to gain their own understandings of their problems and to act on their own understandings?

Finally, now that it is clear that the revolution is still a way off, the question of how to organize the movement for continuing struggle has become important. A tight, disciplined structure like that of JCR is totally incompatible with March 22nd ideals of spontaneity and direct democracy. On the other hand, something as ephemeral as March 22nd will soon disperse (as it has, in large measure, at this writing), into isolated individuals and groups, which will quickly become sectarian or disillusioned. Nevertheless, some people in March 22nd rejected organization or structure of any kind. They have seen too many organizations start out revolutionary and end up in bureaucratic *rigor mortis*. Even the stolid, established CGT began as an association of anarchists. To these modern anarchists, any organization is inherently bureaucratic and hierarchical. The relationship between revolutionaries, like other human relationships, can be killed by being formalized. Spontaneity and independence are what the revolution is about, before and after the destruction of capitalist state power. They are not just goals; they are strategic principles. If you question this view, they point to May, and argue that May will come again, for nothing has been solved. And when it comes again, and yet again, each time May will cast up more people who will live for the next May and the next one, incapable of being satisfied by reformist compromises. To form organizations, they say, would be to defeat oneself, would be to try to channel what must, by its very nature, run free of channels.

Other students believe that May was unique. They argue that for sustained struggle, some kind of organization is needed. They are just as opposed as the others to the traditional kind of left organization, as exemplified by the Communist Party. But, they say, to pose the problems of action and of organization as separate questions is to ask the wrong questions. Organization must reflect the needs of action. Strategy, planning over long periods, coordination—all may be necessary for effective action, and organization may be necessary to accomplish them. But organization must never be an end in itself, with a life of its own, divorced from the exigencies of action. Nor can theory or planning or coordinating be ends in themselves. Organization must be the embodiment of the activity and the will and the needs of those who act. It must grow out of these needs, never shape them. It must be completely fluid, constantly destroying itself and constantly recreating itself to meet the changing needs. Any organization must be decentralized, growing up from the needs of the individual members, says this group of students. The central organization must serve only to coordinate, to supply information, and to perform services for the base. The heart and brains of the organization must remain in the base, not in any central committee.

* * *

Words lie heavy on the March 22nd Movement. No amount of analysis could tell as much about March 22nd revolutionary views as a day in Paris in May or June. Whatever it meant on the world money market, or to NATO, or to Premier Pompidou, May was above all a creative breakthrough, a triumph of imagination. For the first time, thousands of students, after years of the steady discipline of school, dared to dream and to act. Many were serious revolutionaries, but no one was grim. "Distrust sad people," said one graffito! *"La révolution, c'est la joie."* To talk to one of the March 22nd activists was to talk to someone who was high. Only after you had spent some time in an occupied building and developed a contact high of your own could you begin to understand.

The École des Beaux-Arts, renamed by its occupiers the "Ex-École des Beaux-Arts," looked like the scene of some unearthly festival. The black, fortress-like walls were slashed with red flags and covered with posters, slogans, and long passages from the works of various revolutionary heroes. The statues surrounding the courtyard had been painted, decorated, or given red flags to hold. But liberated art isn't all hedonism. Upstairs in the Ex-École, dozens of ex(?)-students worked frantically to get out the day's supply of revolutionary posters, which would appear on the walls in every quarter of Paris the next day. Others were heading off to the factories to talk to the striking workers, or were writing tracts to be handed out all over the city.

At the annex to the faculty of letters at Censier, the walls were covered with poems. In the amphitheaters of the Sorbonne, debate went on into the night. Sundays, thousands of workers crowded into the Sorbonne courtyard to talk with the students. An eyewitness account, published in an English pamphlet on the events, described it like this:

> Those who had never dared say anything suddenly felt their thoughts to be the most important thing in the world—and said so. The shy became communicative. The helpless and isolated suddenly discovered that collective power lay in their hands . . . A tremendous surge of community and cohesion gripped those who had previously seen themselves as isolated and impotent puppets, dominated by institutions they could neither control nor understand. . . . An inscription on a wall sums it up perfectly: *"Déjà dix jours de bonheur"* (Already ten days of happiness).

A year before May, a widely read pamphlet put out by the International Situationists in Strasbourg, said it like this: True proletarian revolution is *"une fête."* "Play is the ultimate rationale of this fête, to live outside of dead time and to act without inhibitions."

The demands of May were only the verbalization of the revolutionary mood. One word sums them all up: *autogestion. Autogestion* translates somewhat pallidly as "self-management," but it can only be defined by examples. In factories, *autogestion* meant control by workers. In schools, it meant control by students and teachers (assuming, of course, that the old hierarchical student-teacher relationship would be destroyed, and that teachers and students would study together.) In the family, it meant an end to patriarchal domination of wives and children. In fact, in any institution involving more than one person, *autogestion* meant direct democratic control by everyone involved. The mechanisms of control need not be carefully prescribed, since they would be flexible and changing with the needs and interests of the participants. However, they should never be merely representational—the quickest way to give up power is to hand it over to a representative. Direct democracy, direct participation in all decision-making is the key.

This demand for *autogestion,* the style of struggle, the attitudes toward organization and toward organizing together define the utopia of the students. Revolution to them was not to be just a transfer of power, but an *end* to power, a freeing of people to grow and to do what it is possible for them to do, as more and more *becomes* possible. There was no talk of "when we run society. . . ."—society is not something to be "run" but something to be participated in. The utopia "after the revolution" is the continuation of the revolution, the continual opening up of new ways to be human. To quote Cohn-Bendit once more: "It isn't a matter of . . . figuring out how to make 'the revolution'. . . . We are moving toward a perpetual change in society, spurred on, at each stage, by revolutionary actions."

How much of these ideals, this spirit, was shared by the workers is problematical. The vast majority of the workers remained loyal to the trade unions and to the Communist Party throughout. But at many stages it is clear that it was the workers who were leading, not the unions. The workers' movement did not erupt because the workers were led by students, but because the conditions of their own lives led them to revolt. The workers were particularly oppressed in France. The work week was the longest in the Common Market countries, and wages were second lowest. The economy was growing rapidly, and consumer goods were becoming more and more available, but workers were not getting their full share of the new prosperity. Wage increases lagged far behind overall economic growth.

French employers range from feudally paternalistic to outright reactionary in their relations with employees, both in the factory and through the government apparatus. As a result of all these factors, months of bitter wildcat strikes preceded the May uprising. In this context, the students did not function by organizing workers around workers' issues. They pursued their *own* demands, setting the example of unabashed, self-interested militancy. The workers followed the students' example.

The contacts between students and workers which followed were individual and spontaneous. We have told earlier how after the great procession on the first day of the general strike, students and workers mingled through the evening on the Champ de Mars. In the battles on the barricades, too, many young workers had joined in, battling the police side by side with the students. These battles gave the students a certain credibility in the eyes of the workers; they were willing to risk themselves, they were serious, not just *fils de papa*, "papa's boys." As the general strike developed, the students went out to the occupied factories, to help the workers. The workers, in turn, came by thousands to the Latin Quarter, to see what the students were doing. The students' mystique and romanticism about industrial workers for once stood them in good stead. The workers could talk their minds, and the students, even if they disagreed, listened carefully. Gratified by the respect and friendship of so many "intellectuals," many workers returned again and again. When the discussions got more serious, the workers and students often found that they still had great difficulty in communicating; their expectations and modes of thought were too different. But the emotional bonds had been created.

The students also provided concrete assistance to the striking workers. They organized peasants to provide food for the strikers in return for services. This was important in France where unions have no strike funds. At Flins, at the big Renault plant, students joined the workers in battling the police who attempted to reoccupy the factory. Students also set up meeting places for workers, where for the first time workers could talk to other workers about the conditions of their lives, free from the restraining influence of the unions. For example, they brought together transit system workers from different depots in Paris. When the workers began to compare notes, they learned for the first time of the ways in which the CGT leaders had manipulated each depot to get them to end their strike.

But after June, the contacts remaining were slim. It is unclear how much of the revolutionary passion of the students was transmitted to the workers. Perhaps the workers will be satisfied for now with the wage increases and improved working conditions they won in May. Even the future of the student movement is uncertain at the time of this writing. By August, student plans for "summer universities" for workers had almost completely fallen apart under the weight of stepped-up police repression (and summer vacations). According to March 22nd people, March 22nd itself was drifting apart. The noisier ones had been arrested, and the quieter ones had disappeared.

Back in June, a March 22nd activist told us that the students might not be able to carry through the revolution, might even become counter-revolutionary. "But it doesn't matter," he continued, "because the sixteen-year-olds, the thirteen-year-olds, are revolutionary now. They will push us out of the way and go on by themselves someday."

CHAPTER SIX

England: The Silent Spring

I used to get mad at my school
The teachers that taught me weren't cool
You're holding me down, turning me round
Filling me up with your rules.
I've got to admit it's getting better
A little better all the time. . . .

—Beatles

French students were tossing Molotov cocktails from behind the barricades and German students were storming Springer Verlag, and a few hundred miles away, in England, the English Left looked on admiringly. Spring did bring England its own tentative burgeoning of student unrest. But is was with obvious strain that the English press tried to find analogies to the Sorbonne in the gentlemanly occupations of English art colleges. By all rights, they seemed to be saying, England should have a student revolution of its own. After all, England is the historic educational capital of the West, attracting thousands of students from all over the world. In the last few years England has even been an international center of youth culture, drawing mods and heads from all the former colonies. Furthermore, England has a sturdy tradition of student leftism dating back to the Suez crisis and the Committee for Nuclear Disarmament. England had all this and no movement. There were activities, but the issues and their adherents remained cleanly separated.

Unlike France or Italy, England has no tradition of any specific *student* consciousness. The pre-1968 history of student-power struggles in England is confined to one major incident, the occupation of the London School of Economics in 1967. LSE was a natural focus of trouble. Set up by the Fabian Society (a socialist intellectual circle, whose heyday was in the pre-World War I period) for students unable to afford Oxford or Cambridge, LSE attracts older students, leftists, and foreigners, including many Americans. None of them were pleased when the administration chose the Principal of University College in Rhodesia, Dr. Walter Adams, as the new director of LSE. Adams, the students believed, had played a key role in effectively compromising the Rhodesian university with the racist Smith regime.

Probably the agitation over Adams's appointment would have remained verbal had the administration not been so inept: in January 1967, as interest in Adams's appointment was already beginning to flag, some students planned a teach-in on the subject in a university room. Less than an hour and a half before the meeting was scheduled to begin, the administration forbade the use of the room for the meeting. When several hundred students gathered in protest, the director of LSE told them, "Students have no rights. . . ." In the uproar that followed, the students decided to hold the meeting as scheduled. After weeks of legalistic deliberation, the administration responded by suspending two of the student leaders, Marshall Bloom and David Adelstein. The original causes of student irritation were almost entirely overshadowed by this display of administrative willfulness. Bloom is an American, and a suspended American was the closest thing England had to a Vietnam-bound draftee. Five hundred students began a week-long sit-in in the LSE buildings.

The sit-in never made much progress beyond the disciplinary issue. General issues, even university problems other
than the current suspensions, received little concerted attention. Only on the fifth day, with negotiations practically in
sight, were seminars and counter-courses even proposed. On
the seventh day, the occupiers voted to leave and, very peacefully, left. (A few months later, the sit-in was vindicated by
an administration decision to reinstate Bloom and Adelstein.) The British *New Left Review* (May-June, 1967)
hailed the LSE action as a breach in the "undergraduate
complex" and the beginnings of a "collective *student* consciousness," but many of the participants were less impressed.
The moderate students felt that they had made their point,
and made it with plenty of time left to prepare for exams.
The leftist students were largely disheartened by the anti-
climactic conclusion to the sit-in, and felt that they had gone
"too far" for too little. Richard Kuper, a leader of the sit-in,
wrote in 1968: "One of the paradoxical results of the sit-in
during the last academic year is that although it ended in victory on the issue of victimisation, it has led many militant
socialists to a total rejection of student activity in favor of
work in other fields."

* * *

The nearest other field, strangely enough, was Vietnam.
Many militant students were attracted to the Vietnam Solidarity Committee, which transcended the pacifism of the
Committee for Nuclear Disarmament to declare support for
the NLF. Originally headed by Bertrand Russell, VSC moved
steadily out from under him and to the left. By the spring
of 1968, Oxford's flamboyant militant, Tariq Ali, was the
acknowledged leader of VSC. Along with milder English

peace groups, VSC helped mobilize thousands for a march during the October 1967 International Protest Days, which had been called by the U.S. National Mobilization Committee. In March 1968, VSC and other militant groups more or less lit out on their own. A march climaxed at the American Embassy in Grosvenor Square, where the frustrated students managed to provoke some skirmishes with the bobbies. The English students were not used to violence, and the few American demonstrators present were not used to having to provoke it.

The militance displayed at Grosvenor Square and at LSE *was* somewhat out of place in England. In every country in Europe where student protests have moved beyond legality, the press is quick to uncover foreign instigation. In England there was actually a good deal of truth to the charge that the militance was imported. For instance, at LSE, the American Bloom and the South African Adelstein were not just passive martyrs of the sit-in; they were leaders. And if the rank and file contained no more American radicals than the LSE student body generally, there would still have been enough of them around to keep the legend of Berkeley alive. As for Vietnam, the English are not only indebted to us for the issue, but for many of the tactics and analyses it engendered. Many of the English Vietnam activities were inspired by activities in the U.S., and were energetically supported by American activists in England. The Stop-It Committee (Americans in Britain for U.S. Withdrawal from Vietnam) has been influential out of all proportion to its size. Stop-It research, implicating English universities and industries in the Vietnam war effort and demonstrating U.S. domination of English industry (and often of English government), helped make anti-imperialism a little less abstract in the former Empire.

But the imported militance on Vietnam and student power

has not yet fully taken root in English student consciousness. When Frankie Y, an indigenous black-powerite, demanded of a student meeting, "How many of you can shoot a gun?" the audience tittered, and someone yelled back, "Why should we?" Indeed, even the police are unarmed. So far, the English attitude toward the student "revolutionaries" has been disarmingly benevolent. For example, in the spring of 1968, while nearby countries were discouraging tourism by any-one under thirty, the BBC (the national television network) *invited* a bevy of foreign leftist student leaders to London. The CIA must have ogled in disbelief as they arrived: SDS from Germany, SDS from New York, March 22nd from Paris, the student underground from Spain, the "movement" from Rome, etc. The English loved it. For a few days, Yugo-slavia's lovely Dragana Stavajiel and France's Dany Cohn-Bendit edged Princess Margaret off front pages of women's magazines and daily newspapers. A newspaper cartoon showed a buxom Mother England embracing sullen Tariq Ali and Dany Cohn-Bendit. Ali is saying, "Well, Dany, how do we start a revolution in this atmosphere?" The fires of re-bellion are easily doused by the lukewarm tea of English tol-erance.

But there is perhaps a more important reason why English soil has been barren ground for the growth of a mass student movement. Compared to many European countries, Eng-land has found a sort of solution to the problems of higher education. English education is strictly divided, by class and by function. The ancient universities, Oxford and Cam-bridge and to a certain extent London University (with which LSE is affiliated), are the elite institutions. Tradition-ally the place where scions of the aristocracy learned to hold their liquor, "Oxbridge" takes upper- and upper-middle-class youths and turns them out as executives, Parliamentarians, or

academicians. The less appealing task of producing technicians and teachers is left to the lower class institutions—polytechs, technical colleges, teaching schools, and colleges of art
and commerce. These have shot up entirely since the Industrial Revolution (mostly in the last fifty years) and service
the lower- and middle-class youth. Somewhere in between
the two extremes are a few very new comprehensive universities, which are more analogous to the American multi-purpose university. These have not yet made any substantial
impact on Britain's two-class, or "Binary System" of education.

English students may not be too happy about this bifurca-
tion of the educational system, but, at least, they cannot
complain like the Italians, that the *university* channels its
students into classes. In England, the channeling takes
place much earlier—the college or university is guiltless. Sim-
ilarly, English students cannot claim to have been defrauded
by the kind of education they receive. If all you want is a job,
you go to the appropriate college and learn the requisite
skills, without being burdened by a lot of unnecessary culture. If it is culture you're after, you can go to a university
and completely forget that the world outside holds any such
mundane prospects as "jobs."

England had what may have been its last twinge of guilt
about the Binary System in 1963. At that time a government-
sponsored report (the Robbins Report) on higher education
criticized the *de facto* segregation of students by social class.
The Labour Government's response has been to make the
segregation *de jure*. The problem, as they saw it, was not to
end class discrimination, but to produce, as cheaply as possible, enough technicians for English industry. The colleges
and polytechs were obviously going to have to be the source
of these technicians, because they are public property. Uni-

versities, on the other hand, although they are supported by state grants, are not accountable to the state. The solution then was not to end the Binary System, but to entrench it ineradicably. The Coldstream Reform in 1965 dignified the colleges with a special "degree" of their own, wistfully conceived to be equivalent to a university degree. Adelstein of LSE wrote that the government hoped to "encourage a technocratic ethos of sufficient status to rival the university tradition . . . to break the old liberal stranglehold of the university and replace it with a new managerial-technological culture." Decked out with their new degree and a smattering of "academic" courses for the masses, the colleges were supposed to hold their own as proud younger brothers of the universities. No one, of course, was much fooled.

* * *

By international standards, very little radical student activity happened in England this spring. What did happen was about as carefully segregated along the lines of the Binary System as are the students themselves. The colleges brought forth England's first true student syndicalists, acting on the single issue of educational reform. The universities featured the customary activities of student leftists—agitation on Vietnam, germ warfare, worker (but not student) power—at a pace slightly quickened by the French example.

Ironically, the college activities were a reaction to the Coldstream reforms, rather than to the conditions the reform aimed to change. The rebellion centered in the art colleges—Guilford, Croydon, and especially Hornsey. In every sense, Hornsey is a poor college, with limited space and supplies for a growing number of students of very limited means. The academic trappings imposed by Coldstream must have seemed unsuitable from the start, but as time went on they became intolerable. In the first place, the "reformed" entrance requirements, a series of written exams, have no predictive value for artistic ability. Having struggled over those hurdles, the art student faced time-consuming academic courses which had no relevance to his development as an artist. He had little choice of curriculum once having settled on one of the arbitrary divisions of art—"fine art," "design," etc.—as a major. In fact, art students came to feel that if they developed as artists, they did so in spite of their education. In order for the students to learn art, they felt, either they or the staff would have to leave college.

At Hornsey, the students decided to stay. On May 29, irritated by a dispute over funds for the student union, close to half the student body occupied the college buildings. The administration simply vanished. For the first two weeks the occupiers discussed art education day and night, issuing scores of documents, letters to high government officials, and leaflets for the local townspeople. Art is a lonely business and many of the students had never met each other, much less realized they had the same problems. Delighted in their new-found community, they declared themselves "members" (not students) of the Hornsey College of Art and began to run it themselves. They put on art shows and offered night courses for the local taxpayers, who, in turn, expressed their support with petitions and letters to Parliament.

Throughout the "Hornsey revolution" the students made every effort to preserve a respectable public image. "Liquor and licentiousness" were barred from the occupied buildings. Better yet for the public eye, they steered clear of that most disreputable student vice—politics. At the start of the occupation, the Communist-leaning student union president was retired to a less conspicuous rank-and-file position.

When the members of the sectarian International Socialist organizations appeared at Hornsey, eager to recruit from the occupying ranks, they were unceremoniously thrown out. The Hornseyites even rejected financial support offered by a Trotskyist printers' union. In their own discussions, they rarely trespassed beyond art education issues to general educational issues and to problems of the society as a whole. (There was sometimes a tendency to become more political. For example, after several weeks of occupation, some *New Left Review* people were invited to speak at Hornsey. Also, for some students there was a cultural if not ideological identification with student revolutions elsewhere, with the myth of Che, etc. We were told that at some other art colleges where occupations occurred, such as Croydon, the rejection of "politics" was not as great as at Hornsey.)

All in all, the Hornsey rebels' policy of apolitical purity paid off in widespread public support. The English liberal press was considerably kinder to the Hornseyites than the French Communist press was to the *enragés* of Nanterre. Police violence or administrative retaliation hardly seemed to be serious threats. When we asked some Hornsey students what they would do if the electricity were turned off, we were told, "It would be a national scandal if they turned off the power. It would be inhumane!"

In maintaining their apolitical purity, the Hornsey students were not timidly evading the "real" issues to keep out of trouble. Nor did they have some Machiavellian plan to preserve a lowest-common-denominator line which would appeal to students in other colleges. In fact, they *were* apolitical. Despite all the governmental attempts to upgrade art education, art schools are by and large trade schools, and art students are not intellectuals. The Hornsey intonation was more Cockney than Cambridge, and the style was exuberantly mod, not tweed. To these students, deep moral concerns about "the workers" or Vietnam were definitely luxury items. They had a narrow set of demands which they personally had to win, which they seriously believed they could win. In fact, the demands raised this spring at Hornsey and other colleges are probably narrow enough to be granted without in any way disturbing the framework of English higher education. A high government official agreed with the rebels that "art education is a mess."

It seemed almost certain that if the students continued to push, the government would find a way to reform its past reforms, and the students would be free to get back to work. So far, then, the student power thrust in England is not an open-ended challenge to authoritarianism, but is primarily a trade-union type of demand for recognition. In fact, when the Hornsey administration returned to negotiate in July, it hardened its approach, and coupled its peace offers with threats of repression. After six weeks of occupation, the majority of the students, faced with these threats, decided to accept peace terms involving the establishment of a joint student-staff committee to discuss the problems of art education. Since then, there have been signs that college administrators and local government officials are preparing to crack down on student unrest. As a result, pure student unionism may find itself forced to become more and more political.

* * *

The other stream of English extra-curricular activity centers in the universities, home of the left-intellectual tradition. Like the Fabian Society before them, the student socialist groupings are not massive, but have a remarkable ability to survive long periods of inaction. There are ex-Labourites, disenchanted by the present government, International Socialists (about three hundred altogether), members of the campus Socialist Societies numbering around one thousand nationally, Communists, and various detached Maoists, Guevarists, etc. None of these groups resembles anything an American would recognize as "New Left." Although their organizations consist almost wholly of students, and university students at that, these leftists have always been a little uncomfortable about being students. To raise student demands would only make a point of their embarrassing condition. Nevertheless, university leftists have made occasional forays into university issues.

In the winter of 1966-67, they surfaced as the Radical Student Alliance (RSA) with hopes of supplanting the established National Union of Students (NUS: equivalent to the American National Student Association, complete with ties to the CIA-funded International Student Conference). RSA's initial drive was in opposition to the hike in fees for foreign students, but in the backwaters of English college education, this issue roused little excitement. NUS continued, undisturbed, on its smug, bureaucratic path. The RSA experience only confirmed the conviction of many student radicals that students were not really worth the attention of radicals. Early in 1968, Richard Kuper of LSE wrote, "to build a socialist student movement is a worthy objective; unfortunately it requires socialism first."

But events of the spring convinced many of the left students that socialism might be a long time coming. Enoch Powell, a reactionary member of Parliament, made a speech denouncing the coming inundation of England by blacks from various parts of the commonwealth. When liberals moved to censure him, the dock workers held a demonstration in massive support for Powell's white-power sentiments.

Now the dockers have always been one of the most militant, even leftist, trade unions in England. Imagine the left sectarians' chagrin when these workers booed down an anti-racist International Socialist speaker.

If the Powell incident did not exactly cure student romanticism about the workers, it certainly demonstrated the shakiness of the Left's "base" in the working class. Roused by fears of "fascism," many left groups began to look for allies in liberal organizations, in peace groups, and even, once again, among their fellow students. Events in France, Germany, and Italy accelerated the Left's re-evaluation of students as a constituency. In early June 1968, radicals at LSE decided that England, too, needed a mass left-wing student movement. So they called for one:

> British students this year have watched their counterparts abroad make history. . . . What are the prospects for militant students in Britain? So far the beginnings of student struggle have been encouraging but scattered. . . . The LSE Socialist Society has recently taken an important intitiative by *calling for* a revolutionary student movement. Such an organization answers an urgent need. (From the call for the founding convention of the Revolutionary Socialist Students Federation; emphasis added.)

On June 14-16, about a thousand students, mainly members of campus Socialist Societies, showed up at LSE for the founding convention of the Revolutionary Socialist Students Federation (RSSF). Proudly hailed by the liberal British press as "Britain's first equivalent to the German SDS and American SDS," RSSF obviously had a lot of work on its hands. But a faction cannot create an organization, any more than an organization can create a movement. Every detail of the temporary constitution of RSSF and the composition of the summer interim coordinating committee went through the deadening mill of parliamentary procedure.

Even the name took endless factional dispute, equally divided between discussion on "revolutionary," "student," and "federation," with only "socialist" winning almost unanimous accord. For every factional opinion, there was a leaflet and usually a counter-leaflet or two.

After all the revolutionary rhetoric, the most alienated people at the meeting were those who came without either a supporting faction or a printing press, ordinary students on the verge of being left, or left-out. One student we talked to was less concerned about socialism than about the retake of final exams in sociology, ordered (unfairly, he thought) by the university after some cheating had been uncovered. "I was dying to organize some action," he said. "I thought that's what revolutions are all about. But they just like to talk."

Now all this was occurring, not only in the same country, but at the same time as rebellion was sweeping the art colleges. Yet when it came to student actions, it was hard to tell whether the RSSF people were less interested in the "student" or the "action" part.

While movements in other countries have relied almost exclusively on direct action, such as occupations, the English leftists have little use for action in a theoretical void: "Given the correct line, the correct tactic will follow," they told us. They either do not see, or do not see how to use, confrontation as a means of raising consciousness and creating "the line." As for student demands, attitudes ranged from indifferent to contemptuous. Their only obeisance to student power was to tack it on to the call for the RSSF meeting as an issue, but it looked like an afterthought. When we asked an RSSF organizer what he thought of the student-power types in the colleges, he dismissed them in a sentence: "They're just student syndicalists." The leftists are not interested in reforming the universities and they see no way of radicalizing the struggle for reform. For instance, an LSE socialist wrote that student demands "may lead to more involvement and more moral indignation when they aren't realized, but is this sort of cynicism what we really want?" In general, to these student leftists, students may be valuable agents for activating workers, but students themselves are uninteresting: student issues are hopelessly bourgeois.

Ironically, one month of college occupations probably produced more student-worker contacts than a year of leftist leafletings. For instance, at Guilford College of Art, guards hired to besiege the occupied buildings defected to the side of the students, because they decided that the students were right and because they realized they had some gripes of their own.

* * *

For all their differences in form and content, style and theory, the student powerites and the student socialists seemed to us to have certain attitudes in common. The American movement has always insisted on the importance of knowing its enemy and making its friends. The English students were somewhat at a loss on both counts. Neither group seemed to have any firm notion of where power really lies, of who or what the enemy really is. From Hornsey, the rebels faced a vague hierarchy of education authorities, divided vertically and horizontally and involving both the local and national governments. From the first day of the occupation, when the administration fled the college, the students were never able to push the conflict to a clear confrontation with some responsible agency or official.

The leftist students, taking on all of "capitalism," seemed to have an even harder time pinpointing authority. Certainly their universities, the mass media, and most Parliamentarians were benign enough. To the International Socialists, the threat is now "fascism," as if they were searching for some concrete form to give the unknown enemy.

As for making friends for the cause, neither student grouping seems to have much respect for the American movement byword—organizing. For instance, the left sectarians seemed to consider leafleting at plant gates to be "organizing." Going to work or live with workers was never mentioned. In the colleges, this problem was even more acute. At a meeting on college education at Hornsey, someone from a nearby polytech suggested pushing for "one man—one vote" as the principle by which colleges should be run. Everyone objected: If issues were decided on a one man—one vote basis, "we might lose." When we asked the students why they didn't consider the possibility of working to win over the majority of students in, say, polytechs, the answers indicated that the question was almost meaningless: "But they (the other students) don't agree with us." Perhaps it is ungentlemanly to try to change someone else's mind.

* * *

Nothing could be easier than analyzing the "failings" of a non-movement, since anything you say is bound to be right. To us, England was primarily interesting for the perspective it gave us on what happened last spring in other countries. In Italy, France, and Germany, university problems, aggravated by every governmental "reform," growing more acute with every incoming wave of freshmen, ran headlong into the fact of Vietnam. If doctors, teachers, and technicians are cogs in the system and Vietnam is a product of the system, then why live in poverty and degradation for ten years to become doctor, teacher, or technician? The disparity between the liberal ethos dished out at the university and the increasing proletarianization of students, for increasingly suspect purposes, was unbearable.

In England, the Binary System of education did not solve these problems, but it did separate them. University students felt one set of problems, and college students another. University students, nurtured on vintage liberal arts ethos, reacted morally to Vietnam, but the indignation did not spill over into any problems of their own lives. As a matter of fact, they would be hard pressed to say what their problems are. University students in England are not treated like a faceless mass of mental retardates. They are "gentlemen taught by gentlemen," on their way to being gentlemen and scholars. As institutions the universities seem unimpeachably autonomous: unaccountable to the government and unaccountable *for* the government. Their function is not to cater to the immediate needs of government and industry, but to "fuse teacher and taught in the unfettered quest for wisdom."

None of this for the lowly college students. They are being trained for a job. When the training effort stumbled on the college's new liberal arts pretensions, as at Hornsey, the students rebelled. Theirs was not so much a strike as a back-to-work drive against the newly imposed academic courses and cultural frills. Which is more important to a commercial artist, they were asking, Picasso or plastics technology? When jobs are hard to come by, as in England now, the choice is clear. College and technical students should no more be blamed for failing to rebel over Vietnam and the imperialist functions of their trade than should the English dockers. Collegiate education does not cultivate, and post-collegiate jobs do not encourage, such refined sensitivities. If college students

seemed overly involved in their own problems, it is because
they are subject to direct oppression: over-crowded classrooms, inadequate facilities, immediate poverty, and factory-
style education. If they fail to relate their own problems to
those of the Vietnamese, the Biafrans, etc., which so move
the university leftists, we blame the university leftists, for
their inability to relate to the immediate problems of lower-
class students.

We can't help wondering, along with the RSSF founders:
What *are* the prospects for militant students in Britain? Have
student tensions really been defused by the Binary System?
At least one element of the English Left (the only recognizable "New Left") thinks not. *New Left Review* and May
Day Manifesto people (these are early thirtyish intellectuals,
veterans of the Committee for Nuclear Disarmament) point
out that the problems of English higher education, like the
problems of England generally, are getting worse faster than
the Labour government can patch things up. First, the number of students is growing much faster than the number of
seats in lecture halls. The English student population ex-
ploded from 70,000 before World War II to 216,000 in 1962
and to 300,000 in 1965: from 2.7 per cent of the age-group in
1939 to 11 per cent in 1967. While student population growth
accelerates, the number of available jobs seems to be actually declining. In June we read a human interest story in a
London newspaper about two chemistry grads who had finally landed jobs—as personnel managers! English brains
don't just drain away, they're practically driven to Route
128 or Highway 66 for jobs. Even the conservative NUS demanded this spring that "government and college authorities
should provide more effective career advice to all students."
Colleges adjust to the tightening job market by doing their

best to limit the number. Exams, "spaced so as to give students nervous breakdowns," were blamed for a couple of suicide attempts during the few days we were in England.

Meanwhile, the government has fewer and fewer of its new, lightweight pounds to gamble on the strained educational system. Everyone, especially the workers, wants a larger cut of the pie, which is getting smaller all the time. The government has decided to limit its increase for educational spending to 5 per cent per year, although students are increasing by about 15 per cent per year. Among other things, this has meant that scholarship grants have not kept pace with the cost of living. Many English students are living on less than $14 a week, of which $7 is for rent, and English food is not as cheap as the taste suggests.

If things keep going the way they have been, this chapter should soon find its place in the prehistory of the English student movement. How soon is almost a matter of arithmetic.

CHAPTER SEVEN

Columbia: Up Against the Ivy Wall

A university is definitely not a democratic institution.
When decisions begin to be made democratically around
here, I will not be here any longer.

—Herbert Deane,
Vice Dean of the Graduate Faculties,
Columbia University, April 24, 1967

The main thing we learned is that things can change.
—Columbia Strike Committee Leaflet

The most far-reaching student explosion in the United
States up to this writing was at Columbia University in New
York City in the spring of 1968. Thousands of students, led
by the radical Students for a Democratic Society (SDS) seized
control of part of the campus for a week and then shut down
the entire university for the remainder of the semester. The
press invoked all sorts of causes: the ineptitude of Columbia's administration under President Grayson Kirk, the distance between faculty and students, the archaic organization of the university power structure itself. Rarely did the
press recall that there were issues at Columbia, issues which
students had been fighting over for more than two years before the blow-up. Rarely did it admit that there were more
students involved over this two-year period than a few dozen
extremists led by the "ruthless" Mark Rudd.

Radical activity became significant at Columbia, as at so

many other American universities, in 1965 with the beginning of the American bombing of North Vietnam. At that time there was no SDS chapter at Columbia. The organizations which could be considered the predecessors of Columbia SDS—the Independent Committee on Vietnam (ICV) and the local CORE chapter—directed their anti-war and anti-racist activities primarily at extramural targets. Columbia CORE demonstrated at the New York World's Fair, helped organize rent strikes, and became active in the Maryland Freedom Union. ICV sent hundreds of students to Washington for the first of the giant anti-war demonstrations, in April 1965. In the summer and fall ICV started taking the anti-war campaign to the community, through door-to-door canvassing and extensive leaflettings. In these early months of the bombing of Vietnam, the university itself served largely as a kind of neutral territory for meetings, discussions and teach-ins. It first became the scene, if not the target, of an anti-war demonstration in the spring of 1965, when a hundred students demonstrated against Columbia's Naval ROTC program.

By the fall of 1966, many student activists had come to believe that the war in Vietnam was no accident, and that racism was not a matter of individual psychology. Imperialist wars and racism were, they believed, essential features of capitalism. If the issues were related, then there was no point to having ICV deal with one and CORE with the other. They felt the need for a multi-issue organization which could make the connections clear and build a mass movement around them. The occasion soon arose. In November 1967, several hundred students participated in a protest against CIA recruiting on campus. To the students' protest, President Kirk calmly retorted, "It is not desirable, it is not feasible, it is not possible for the University to attempt to make a value judgment about any division of the federal government." The students were already beginning to understand how many "value judgments" were hidden behind this supposed moral neutrality. In the wake of the CIA protest, Columbia SDS was founded. One of its goals was "to expose and attack the political nature of the university." Another was to build a mass movement for "social transformation."

SDS rapidly became the leader of campus radical activity. In February 1967, the CIA returned to campus to recruit. Eighteen students sat-in to prevent them from going about their work. To avoid a scene, the university planned to hold closed disciplinary hearings for the eighteen. About 200 students marched on Kirk's office to demand open hearings. In April the confrontations continued, this time with the Marines. Several hundred students showed up to taunt the Marine recruiters in front of John Jay Hall. A band of right-wing students attacked them. After order was restored, the atmosphere was still too tense for efficient recruiting. The next day, 200 right-wing and 800 left-wing students turned out and confronted each other over hastily erected barricades. There were scuffles, but no serious fighting.

The most important event of that spring, however, was SDS's quiet discovery of the Institute for Defense Analysis (IDA). In 1955, at the prompting of the Secretary of Defense, a group of universities set up IDA as a non-profit, membership corporation. IDA's members were universities and its trustees were university administrators and businessmen. The Department of Defense saw IDA as a means of overcoming, or at least softening, academic scientists' distaste for military research. IDA operates as a clearing house for university warfare research, determining what research is needed, who can do it, and at what university it can best be done. Although it specializes in the evaluation of new weapons systems, IDA has adapted to the shifting preoccupations of the Department of Defense. In the 1950's, nuclear warfare was high on the list. In the 1960's IDA turned to counter-insurgency, doing research on topics like "Chemical Control of Vegetation in Relation to Military Needs."

More recently still, it has turned to problems of domestic pacification with such reports as "Non-Lethal Weapons for Domestic Law Enforcement Officers" and "Evaluation of Selected Present and Potential Poverty Programs." In 1960, Columbia enlisted as a member university of IDA and Grayson Kirk joined its Board of Trustees. Columbia trustee William Burden (a director of such arms-oriented companies as Lockheed Aviation and Allied Chemical) took the key position of Chairman of the IDA Executive Committee.

Columbia's membership in IDA was shrouded in secrecy. In March 1967, at a faculty smoker, Dean of the Graduate Faculties Ralph Halford told a questioner that "Columbia University has no institutional connection with the Institute for Defense Analysis." One week later, the Columbia *Spectator,* the student newspaper, revealed that Columbia had, in fact, been a member since 1960. Dean Halford responded, according to the *Spectator,* by saying that "these things are not in the purview of faculty or students." To the radical students, however, the IDA link was not to be dismissed so lightly. Up to now their concern with the war in Vietnam had been expressed in attacks on institutions *outside* the university. Even in attacking Dow recruiters or Marine recruiters on campus, they were only arguing that the university shouldn't cooperate with these institutions, not that the university itself was guilty. But in IDA, the university was caught red-handed. Actually Columbia's involvement in the war effort took many forms beside IDA membership. A brilliant report published by the North American Congress on

Latin America has pointed out that 46 per cent of Columbia's total budget in 1966 came from government contracts and that over one quarter of this consisted of classified defense contracts. Countless other connections between Columbia institutions and various phases of American foreign policy were documented, from CIA involvement in the School of International Affairs to Business School training programs for managers of America's imperial expansion. IDA was just another of the university's links with the war, but it came to stand for all of them. On April 24, 1967, SDS first demanded that Columbia disaffiliate from IDA.

Students returned to school in the fall of 1967 to learn the administration's response to the unrest of the previous year. Since so many of SDS's activities had involved marching into Kirk's office with a petition, or disrupting recruiting in a university building, Kirk banned all indoor demonstrations. SDS, in turn, demanded the repeal of the ban and immediately proceeded to ignore it by demonstrating inside Low Library against Columbia's involvement with the military. The administration was not yet ready to force a confrontation, though, and the demonstrations continued. A never-ending series of leaflets, teach-ins, meetings in dormitories on student grievances, and room-to-room anti-war canvassings in the dorms filled the winter. There was one demonstration in October when SDS found out that the School of International Affairs had secret contracts with the CIA.

SDS turned next to the issue which was to join IDA in detonating the spring uprising. In February 1968, Columbia began to construct a new gym. What was special about this gym was that it was going up in a city park used primarily by residents of neighboring Harlem. Compared to most land in Manhattan, the gym site had been dirt cheap—only $3000 a year for the lease from the city. When the lease was signed in 1961, Columbia had promised that the gym would include facilities for the community, in order to compensate for the loss of park land. It turned out that only fifteen per cent of the gym space was to be for the community. The rest was for Columbia only, even in the summer time. Furthermore, community residents would not even enter by the same door as the Columbia students; a separate back door was provided for them. To get something of the impact of the gym plans, go back over the last few lines and read "blacks" for community and "whites" for Columbia.

In 1966, the new city park commissioner lit into Columbia for this grab of city park land, and community pressures against the gym began to mount. All of the local elected officials opposed the gym as did many community groups and, increasingly, the students at Columbia. In the face of the growing opposition, Columbia's only concession was to add a small swimming pool to the community part. When construction began, the students and the community cooperated in a series of demonstrations against the gym. Columbia ignored the protests except to press charges against the twenty-six people arrested at the various demonstrations.

What IDA had done for the war, the gym did for racism. Racism was no longer an attribute of some distant, anonymous institutions. Columbia University was racist. Maybe the administration really thought it was doing a good thing for the community by building the gym. Maybe inferior facilities for the community and indifference to community protest were just lapses of taste. But the gym was just one example of Columbia's bulldozer approach to the community. Through the years it had followed a policy of pushing poor people, often black or Puerto Rican, out of the neighborhood by buying up land, demolishing buildings, raising rents, letting buildings fall into ruins, etc.—the same tactics employed by the most corrupt New York slumlords. Columbia CORE and many community organizations had through the years protested against Columbia's policies as a landlord. Columbia always answered in terms of its need for expansion, but there can be no doubt that getting rid of black people in the neighborhood was a major consideration. According to a statement put out by the "Black Students in Hamilton Hall" during the occupation, Jacques Barzun, then provost of the university, had called Harlem "sinister, dangerous, uninviting . . . enemy territory." A document later found by the occupiers of Kirk's office said:

> Public housing [insures] a built-in population which has not yet reached economic satisfaction and which, to some extent, causes disturbances in the surrounding community. . . . The faculty also requires a safe neighborhood . . . [The University] must hold three principles in mind: (1) no public housing between 110th and 123d Street [Columbia is at 116th], (2) room must be available for institutional expansion, and (3) no single-room-occupancy houses north of 110th Street. [These single-room-occupancies, or SRO's, house the rock-bottom poor in the Columbia neighborhood.]

By early spring in 1968, SDS was beginning to lose patience. Peaceful petitions and protests had about as much effect on Grayson Kirk as they have on Lyndon Johnson. In many students' eyes, the situation had already outgrown peaceful protests anyway. Columbia wasn't just neutral ground, a nice place to spend four years and keep out of the army. It was no more autonomous and "value free" than the Pentagon. Once they might have felt that Columbia was just a little too cooperative, that it had just fallen into bad company. Now they understood that serving imperialism and racist urban programs was what the university was about in the first place.

Meanwhile, draft calls were rising and draft regulations

were changing. More and more seniors realized that they would soon be *in* the war they had always been against. Would they go along, or resist? The new mood of desperation was expressed in the March SDS elections. The newly elected officers were less inclined to the slow, steady educational agitation of the preceding years. They were ready for direct action. And to the old list of targets—Dow, the Marines, the CIA—they added a new one—Columbia University.

Events moved quickly. First the radicals, then the administration, then the radicals, escalated the conflict. On March 19, Colonel Akst of the Selective Service System addressed several hundred students on "The Student and the Draft." In the middle of his talk, six "guerrillas" entered the auditorium, dressed in mock army uniforms and carrying a U.S. flag, toy guns, and other toy weapons. Everyone turned, astonished, to see the singing, yelling invaders. While all eyes faced the rear, a young man in the front row stood up and tossed a lemon meringue pie in the colonel's face. As all gaped in total wonder, the guerrillas escaped through the side exits. The story was spread gleefully through the campus. The selective service system could be attacked after all! With a single squishy blow, the new SDS proved it could make a point without making a speech.

A few days later a letter was sent by SDS demanding disaffiliation from IDA. Kirk declined to answer the letter, because it had no return address! On March 27, 150 students defied the ban on indoor demonstrations by marching into Low Library to present the administration with an anti-IDA petition signed by 1,700 students and faculty members. Kirk's response was to put six students (the "IDA six") on probation: the new chairman and vice-chairman of SDS, three members of the SDS steering committee, and the leader of the Columbia chapter of the Resistance (a leading anti-war group).

A few days later, on April 9, the university held a memorial service for Martin Luther King. Mark Rudd, the SDS chairman, startled the meeting by walking up to the stage, grabbing the meeting and denouncing the proceedings. The service was "a moral obscenity," he said. The same men who were responsible for Columbia's racist policies in Harlem and Morningside Heights, the same men who were prosecuting the 26 non-violent demonstrators who had been arrested at the gym site, were now crying over the assassinated civil rights leader. Then Rudd and forty followers walked out.

* * *

The stage was now set. On April 22, the "IDA six" were placed on disciplinary probation. On Tuesday, April 23, SDS called for a demonstration in the middle of the campus to demand public hearings for the six, an end to IDA and gym construction. At noon about 500 people gathered. They marched on Low Library with a petition. When they got there, they found their way doubly blocked: the administration had locked the doors, and a group of right-wing students had surrounded the building. The right-wingers said they were tired of SDS's trying to "run" the campus. By this time the crowd of petitioners was too big and too angry to just shuffle off home. If they couldn't have an indoor demonstration, they might as well have an outdoor one. So after milling around uncertainly for a few minutes, a large band of demonstrators marched over to the site where the new gym was under construction. At the gym site, the demonstrators started tearing down the chain-link fence surrounding the construction site. The police arrived before much de-construction was accomplished, and, after a scuffle and one arrest, drove back the demonstrators. Dispiritedly, the crowd returned to the main part of campus. Someone suggested that they proceed to Dean Coleman's office in Hamilton Hall. When they got to Hamilton, the dean was out, and milling resumed. As soon as the dean arrived, Rudd demanded that he immediately obtain the release of the person who had been arrested at the gym site. Coleman angrily refused and stalked into his office, followed by the crowd of frustrated SDS'ers. Suddenly the logistics outweighed any plan or lack of plan the demonstrators had: they had seized a building and captured a dean.

The first act of the occupiers was to elect a joint steering committee composed of three SDS'ers, four members of the Student Afro-American Society (SAS) and two "independents." Their first task was to draw up a list of demands. The list they came up with read:

1. The disciplinary action resulting from the March 27 indoor demonstration must be lifted, and no reprisals must be taken against those involved in the current demonstration.

2. Construction of the Columbia gymnasium on Morningside Park must be stopped immediately.

3. All relations with IDA must be severed, including President Kirk's and Trustee Burden's membership on the Executive Board of IDA.

4. The ban on indoor demonstrations must be dropped.

5. All future disciplinary actions should be taken by a bipartite committee of faculty and students after an open hearing in which due process was followed.

6. The University must use its good offices to see that all charges against people arrested at the gym site be dropped.

The first demand, amnesty for those in the present demon-station, was to be a precondition for negotiations on the other points.

Quite soon after the occupation began, David Truman, University vice-president, informed Coleman by telephone that he would meet to discuss the issues with the students if they would release Coleman and come over to Wolman Auditorium to talk. The students realized that at this stage, the captured dean was their trump card in any negotiations. They had no reason, from past experience, to expect good faith from Truman if they walked off and left Coleman. So they replied that if Truman really wanted to talk, he could come to them. Truman refused.

As night went on and a number of black community peo-ple joined the sitters-in in Hamilton, the options open to the students became more serious. The blacks, students and community people, caucused separately from the whites, and proposed that they not only maintain the sit-in the next day, but that they barricade the building, not letting anyone in for their Wednesday classes. This proposal deeply divided the whites. The stakes had been raised much higher than any-one who started out at noon, to petition, could have im-agined. If they were merely sitting-in, even holding the dean prisoner (just as Dow recruiters and CIA recruiters had been held prisoner in other universities before), then they were still staging a protest. They were making specific demands which could be, in principle at least, negotiated. But if they were barricading the building, it was no longer just a pro-test. They were then challenging the *power* of the university administration, the administration of a major capitalist in-stitution. They were protesting not only the specific issues of the moment, but the whole racist and militarist path of the

university. Some students saw it in these terms even at the
time. One girl told us, "I was fed up with moral protests. I
didn't want another sit-in, where you just sit there waiting
for the cops and your punishment." Other students were
swayed by the desire to support the blacks, especially now
that community people had come into the building. But the
majority of the whites were not ready to take the leap and
voted against erecting barricades.

At five A.M., after a long night's debate, the blacks informed the white students that, since they were not going to
be solid in their stand, they would have to leave. Many of
the whites now went home, too tired and depressed to go on.
Others were bitter that they could not remain in Hamilton,
standing "side-by-side with their black brothers." One group,
though, about two hundred strong, decided to take a building of their own and barricade it. Preceded by a small ad-
vance party, they headed straight for the symbol of Kirk's
power—Low Library. They broke down the outer door and
then the door to Kirk's office. As each door broke in, the students gasped, a bit stunned at what they had done. Destruction of property, breaking and entering, come hard to even
the most "revolutionary" middle-class mind. Once inside,
they settled in for what was to be a six-day stay. At the time,
the students in Low had very little idea of what they were
doing or what it could lead to. All they knew was that they
had to do something to support the blacks in Hamilton—they
could not leave them alone and isolated. They had had too
many failures, too many frustrations over the past months,
and especially during the last twenty-four hours. "We ran
from the gym site, we ran from Hamilton, let's not run from
here; let's make a stand," said one student. No one really expected it to be more than a last-ditch stand. During the first
hours, the major topic of discussion was not the political

point of the occupation, but what to do when the police came. Everyone felt that arrests were only hours away.

At 7:30 Wednesday morning, the police came. Most of the students in Low jumped out of the windows and escaped, leaving only a couple of dozen behind. But strangely, the police did not remove these last few students. They were concerned with more important things than politics and protest: they had come to rescue Kirk's Rembrandt painting and television set.

Wednesday dawned rainy and chaotic. At around 9 A.M., students began drifting onto campus. The place was sprinkled with police. Two buildings were occupied. The dean was a prisoner. Something was happening but no one had a very clear idea what. Even the protagonists, the occupiers of the buildings, seemed more concerned about what they would do for breakfast than how they had come to be living in offices and classrooms. As the day went on, one rumor replaced another: the police would release the dean; the students in Low had defaced the Rembrandt and were drinking Kirk's liquor; the blacks in Hamilton were armed and ready to fight; "the people" (of Harlem) were coming to burn the place down.

For the leftist students who had missed the activities of the preceding day or dropped out during the night, Hamilton was the center of activity, and Low was still sort of accidental. They all milled around outside of Hamilton, attracting an outer ring of irritated right-wingers. All day, food was passed in, and garbage was passed out. At one point, a white girl returned from a food-shopping trip with a can of red paint, and started to paint "NO GYM" on Hamilton Hall. As the giant red strokes went up, people gasped or giggled—after all, you don't *paint* a *university* building! Somehow this one act brought the whole situation home to people far more clearly than any leaflet could have. You occupy a building; then it's your building. The right-wingers got the message on the wall, too, and charged the painters. Instantly, black students appeared on a balcony of Hamilton and repulsed the rightists with a blast from a Hamilton Hall fire extinguisher. Occupied Hamilton bore its own explanation, "NO GYM."

Wednesday afternoon and evening, people began to drift back to Low, out of curiosity or out of support. At a mass meeting that night, the students called for a strike against Columbia University. Later in the night, two more buildings were "liberated"—Avery by architecture students and Fayerwether by graduate students of sociology and history.

Thursday was tense. The administration, trying to block outsiders from attending a rally on campus that day, closed off the campus to the public; university ID's were checked at all entrances before one could get in. During the day, the administration announced that at Mayor Lindsay's request, they had "temporarily" halted construction of the gymnasium. At one A.M. Friday morning, yet another building, the Math building, was occupied. In response, the administration informed the faculty, the police would be immediately called in.

Many of the faculty were enraged by this announcement. No matter how you felt about the protest, calling the police was "a shameless violation of the autonomy of the university." One group of faculty members announced that they would prevent violence—police or student—by physically guarding the occupied buildings. That night a group of plainclothesmen sent by the administration to clear Low Library encountered a line of faculty members linked arm in arm. The cops had orders to clear the building, so they charged. Before being called off, they had clubbed at least one faculty member. After this embarrassing episode, the faculty persuaded the administration to hold off on calling the police, to close school on Friday, and to use the weekend for negotiations. (Ironically, in the days that followed, the faculty guards of occupied buildings increasingly played the role of the cops they had objected to. They interposed themselves between those in the buildings and right-wing students outside when violence threatened and served as checkers of ID cards at the campus gates to keep out "outside agitators.")

Meanwhile, in the buildings, a new way of life was developing. As people learned to live with the hourly threat of a police raid, defensive measures became a matter of habit instead of a major preoccupation. When the windows had to be taped to keep out missiles or tear gas grenades, someone volunteered and did it. More time went into the mechanics of survival. Classrooms weren't designed to be lived in, as anyone who has spent any time in one knows. Food, blankets, and medical supplies had to be obtained from outside and distributed among hundreds of occupiers. Communications had to be maintained between buildings, too, and on Friday, a "Strike Coordinating Committee" composed of two representatives from each building was set up.

With all these activities in the background, discussion continued twenty-four hours a day. In Low, one room was reserved for sleeping, one for informal discussions, and one for more formal, high-level discussions in response to the rapidly developing political situation. Topics ranged from substantive analyses of imperialism and racism to tactics: how to deal with the faculty, the administration, right-wing students, and police. There was almost no attempt to structure discussions into anything like the Italian counter-courses. The police would inevitably come soon and interrupt them, so there seemed to be little point in trying to plan or schedule them. Because time was short, discussions were intense; because space was limited, everyone joined in. As community *esprit* developed, the more politically experienced took special pains to get everyone to participate, so decisions would be based on full understanding of the issues. Many previously inactive or apolitical students were taking leading roles by the end of the occupation.

Joining the occupation was not something you did idly, or just out of curiosity. First, it took some determination just to enter one of the occupied buildings, since all the doors were thoroughly barricaded. Inside, every detail of physical existence was a challenge. To share one bathroom and a sleeping room with as many as one hundred and fifty people, to be resigned to eating cheese sandwiches and wearing the same clothes day after day, you had to have a pretty clear idea of why you were there. Then there was the constant fear. Everyone knew the police would eventually show up, and many had a lot to lose when they did. Being thrown out of school could mean being drafted and sent to Vietnam. For most of the occupiers, amnesty wasn't just a theoretical issue; it was a matter of life or death. Of course, you could always walk out of the building and find some safe support activities to do on the outside. But so could everyone else. With every hour of the occupation, you either became more committed to it and to the other occupiers, or you left. Few left.

It wasn't all grimness and torment, of course. In Fayerwether, a couple got married during the occupation. For the Low occupiers, it was funny enough just to be living in Grayson Kirk's inner sanctum. The same hardened revolutionaries who had smashed the doors to enter Low at first hesitated to move his furniture—they might scratch it! Being there in the first place was "trespassing" and almost every move you made was "vandalism" or some form of sacrilege. When a window pole scraped against the ceiling, knocking down a few flakes of plaster, everyone gasped—then laughed. Some people drew the line, though, at searching Kirk's files for documents about IDA or Columbia's plans for Harlem. The others tried to explain that Columbia's wheelings and dealings should be made known to the people whose lives they affected, and went ahead and searched. The searchers were eventually redeemed by the discovery of Kirk's draft card, which they promptly sent back to his draft board. While all this was going on, along with endless discussions of imperialism and *Realpolitik,* one small band of occupiers stayed in a corner night and day playing "Diplomacy."

Even if the occupation had had no political impact, it still would have been the most important experience in the lives of many of the occupiers. The life-style imposed by a university is highly individualized. Exams, term papers, grades all encourage (in fact, require) a selfishly competitive outlook. In the buildings, no *one* could win, no *one* could survive: everyone did or no one did. People thought of their "commune" as you might think of your family. Attachments to the communes ran so deep that no one wanted to change buildings, or leave except for necessities. People began to understand that the conventional, privatized way most people live is not really "natural"—it is only a natural result of the competitive capitalist system. In fighting that system, they were creating and experiencing an alternative kind of society.

Outside, as the first shock at the audacity of the SDS'ers and SAS'ers in occupying the buildings wore off, students and faculty turned to the discussions which were to fill the next days. However threatened right-wing students may have felt, the real challenge of the occupation was to the liberal majority of students. They had to face the idea that their responsibility for the war and racism extended right into their everyday lives as students. What Columbia had to do with IDA, what Columbia had to do with Harlem and Vietnam—these things had to do with every student. The occupation put people on the spot far more than the McCarthy campaign ever had. We heard a fairly typical response from a "clean-for-Gene" type coed outside of Hamilton the first full day of the occupation: "I feel so sheepish." But in all the talk, nothing preoccupied people more than two key questions: Were the SDS and SAS students justified in their tactics, even if their demands were just? And even if the tactics were justified, wasn't the demand for amnesty asking a bit much?

Thursday and Friday were warm and sunny. Thousands sat all day in little clusters on the lawn, waiting and talking. Over and over we heard the same refrain: "I support their demands but I can't support their tactics." There are legitimate means of protest and there are illegitimate ones. Kidnapping a dean, forcibly taking over buildings and preventing students from attending classes and faculty from reaching their offices are illegitimate. The ends cannot justify the means. Otherwise any group of people with a storm-trooper mentality could just try to force the university to do their bidding.

The Strike Coordinating Committee replied that it was no tiny minority trying to force its will on the university community. Thousands of students and others supported their demands as just, and through the years, they had used all the legitimate means to try to get the university to at least reopen the question of the gym and IDA. They asked those who questioned their tactics:

Where were you earlier this year when 400 students marched peacefully into Low Library to present Grayson Kirk a letter asking for disaffiliation with IDA? The official response to this

letter was "we cannot answer because there is no return address." Where was the legitimate means for discussion when
SDS challenged Kirk to debate on IDA and there was no answer
at all? Where were you when peaceful demonstrations were
held at the gym site and the University pressed charges against
a minister for trespassing? And where were you when SDS presented a petition on IDA with 1,700 signatures to the administration and their response was to put the six on disciplinary
probation for marching into their building?

Another statement of the Strike Coordinating Committee
continued the reply: "We are confronted with an administration which is determined to maintain absolute power to rule
Columbia as if it were a medieval fief." And still another leaflet pointed out: "Intellectual support without action is worth
nothing. During the course of the years we acted through
more standard channels . . . and we were rebuffed at every
turn, rudely and irresponsibly. Thus the actions we took
were necessary and just."

Some critics focused on the alleged "violence." For example, the faculty met and voted overwhelmingly to "condemn
the violence, including the occupation of the buildings" and
they attacked the "kidnapping" of Dean Coleman. Others
were more worried about the hour-by-hour possibilities of
violence from the police, from the community, or from right-
wing students. Hundreds of students patrolled in green arm-
bands, determined to maintain peace above all. They urged
the Strike Coordinating Committee to get on with the job of
planning the restructuring of the university, so that incidents like this one would not recur. They counseled immediate reconciliation as the only alternative to riot.

Again the Strike Coordinating Committee replied: When
the administration says, "Let Dean Coleman go," we say, "Let
Fred Wilson [the demonstrator arrested at the gym site] go."
He, too, is held prisoner. A later statement pointed out: The

students do not want violence. It is the university which is responsible for violence and threats of violence—violence against the people of Harlem and of Morningside Heights by expropriating their park; violence against the people of Vietnam by participating in IDA; violence against the students by denying them the right to participate in decisions affecting them and by using the police to coerce students who try to exercise their rights to affect such decisions. Indeed, said the statement, the "substance" of the six demands is a "call on the university to end its violence and threats of violence against students and the community."

Some critics, even those who considered themselves leftists, argued that the tactics were, if nothing else, self-defeating. The university is your last sanctuary for free thought, they said. You must not disrupt or destroy a place dedicated to learning and thinking. But the students in the buildings angrily rejected this concept of the university as obsolete: "The ivory tower has been shattered. No longer can anyone maintain the illusion that Columbia University is detached from the conflicts of the world . . . the achievement of a progressive Columbia requires continuing struggle."

But in the end, all these criticisms and cavillings had to bow before reality. The occupation was a fact. Lines had been drawn: Those who opposed the demands of SAS and SDS were free to attack their tactics. But as the occupation went into its second and third and fourth day, and as it expanded to a third and a fourth and a fifth building, and as right-wing opposition began to assert itself forcefully, those who supported the strike demands were forced to support the occupiers of the buildings.

The question which emerged as the new center of attention was the demand of the striking students for total amnesty. Initially, the demand for amnesty for those participating in the buildings was made as a matter of course. In any industrial strike, one of the demands is always for no reprisals against the strikers or their leaders. Likewise, amnesty was one of the earliest concerns of the demonstrators.

Almost immediately, this point became a center of discussion. Some thought it was inconsistent with the other demands and with the logic of the action. For example, the Columbia *Spectator* announced its support of the demands to end construction of the gym, the ban on indoor demonstrations, and the ties with IDA. But it centered its discussion on mechanisms for ensuring orderly disposition of student grievances and disciplinary matters in the future. It picked up the demand for a bipartite committee of faculty and students to hold open hearings on disciplinary action, and demanded that this mechanism be applied to the current demonstration. Others, who supported the demands and tactics of the occupation, still argued that demanding amnesty weakened the students' moral position. Invoking the classical civil disobedience doctrine of Martin Luther King, they argued that one has the moral right and the moral duty to resist unjust laws or regulations or actions, but that one must be ready to accept punishment for the act of resistance. Civil disobedience should challenge unjust laws, not the authority of the lawmakers.

Even within the occupied buildings, there was growing dissension on the amnesty issue. One group of occupiers raised the tactical point that the demand for amnesty was overshadowing all other issues and obstructing negotiations. The amnesty issue was only confusing the mass of students and alienating the faculty. Almost as a matter of *noblesse oblige*, they felt the Strike Coordinating Committee should drop the amnesty demand and negotiate for meaningful concessions on the *real* issues.

The majority on the Strike Coordinating Committee insisted, however, that all of the arguers against the amnesty
demand were really saying that, although the authorities
might be obstinate and wrong, they were nevertheless the
authorities, and were, *ipso facto,* legitimate. In fact, they said,
the Columbia administration was not legitimate:

> We . . . believe in the right of all people to participate in
> the decisions that affect their lives. An institution is legitimate
> only if it is a structure for the exercise of this collective right.
> The people who are affected by an illegitimate institution have
> the right to change it.
>
> Columbia University has been governed undemocratically.
> An Administration responsible only to the Trustees has made
> decisions that deeply affect students, faculty, and the com-
> munity. It has expropriated a neighborhood park to build a
> gym. It has participated, through IDA, in the suppression of
> self-determination throughout the world. It has formulated
> rules and disciplined students arbitrarily and for the purpose
> of suppressing justified protest. The actions of the Administra-
> tion in the present crisis have exposed it to students and faculty
> as the anti-democratic and irresponsible body it has always
> been.
>
> Our goal is to create a functioning participatory democracy
> to replace the repressive rule of the Administration and Trust-
> ees of this University. The acceptance of amnesty is a funda-
> mental part of this transition because it establishes the ille-
> gitimacy of the existing structure. The granting of amnesty is
> the formal establishment of a new order—the right and power
> of all people affected by the University not to be judged by ille-
> gitimate authority.

Amnesty was, the majority of the occupiers argued, the
central point, not a distraction from the "real" issues. "If we
make concessions, rhetorical or substantive, on amnesty, we
may win in return the granting of other of our demands.
However we lose the essential political point that the administration is illegitimate."

Amnesty was the central issue; it summed up all the oth-

ers. Where you stood on amnesty defined your whole attitude to the university and to the society it serves. To drop
the amnesty demand was to say, in effect: the administration
made a mistake with IDA and the gym. It made an additional
mistake when it ignored legitimate and overwhelming protest. But the administration is legitimate. To be mistake-
proof, the argument continued, the university must be *restructured* to provide smooth channels for dissent. Students
and faculty need a share of the power; how great a share is
subject to negotiation. After a discussion of restructuring,
negotiations should proceed to the immediate issues of the
gym and IDA. As for discipline for the protestors, clemency,
not amnesty, is a reasonable request, since the protestors had
no legal channels of dissent.

On the other hand, to stick to the amnesty demand was
to question the whole function and nature of the university:
What is a university for? To whom is it responsible—the students, the faculty, the community, or the corporate elitists
who sit on the Board of Trustees? Whom does it serve—the
needs of scholars and students or the needs of the military-
industrial complex? Who has power in the university and
how do they use it? Questions on specific programs, like the
gym, might be settled by negotiations, but questions of
power and its uses are only decided by a test of strength.
"Power is never given away, but has to be taken by those
who believe their cause is just." (SDS leaflet).

None of these questions were to be easily resolved, and
meanwhile, the occupation continued. There were constant
rumors of a bust, as the police alternately withdrew and reoccupied the campus. The faculty circled around aimlessly,
trying to understand and control the breakdown of the old
order, but fouling up hopelessly in attempts to follow a
middle course between students and administration. Oppo-

sition groups of students emerged. One such group, calling itself over-hopefully "The Majority Coalition," blockaded Low, trying to starve the occupiers out. Other students, supporters of the occupation, tried to breach their line. Having failed, they threw food up to the occupiers through the windows. The faculty, standing between the occupiers and their besiegers, concerned themselves with such niceties as deciding the exact point beyond which food had to fall for it to be legitimate for the occupiers to lay claim to it.

On Friday, hundreds of black high-school students broke through the police lines and entered the campus, some going into the buildings. Student Non-Violent Coordinating Committee leaders Rap Brown and Stokely Carmichael were literally pulled through the police lines. After discussions with the blacks in Hamilton, they came out and Brown simply read the black students' demands (approximately the same as the Strike Coordinating Committee's six points), and withdrew, saying they were going to get support in Harlem. The fear of Harlem's response, more than anything else, kept the police from intervening for the rest of the weekend. Friday and Saturday were beautiful days, and the campus was crowded with students. People could have drifted off since these were all "holidays," but Columbia was where the action was. Even neutral students felt drawn to the campus and the endless discussions. As one student commented, "I learned more in those few days than in the rest of my time at Columbia."

The university administration alternated threats with slightly more conciliatory remarks. Their key strategy was to work on the blacks, trying to split them from the whites (whom they virtually ignored). They warned the blacks that the whites were only using them, and would betray them in the end. Then they offered the blacks amnesty for the blacks only, along with concessions on the gymnasium issue. The blacks refused the offers and stood with the whites and the common demands.

Finally, Monday night. The police and the administration had at last decided that there was little danger that Harlem would rise up to defend the students. They waited until late at night, until the exact hour when they calculated that Harlem would go to bed, and then moved in. The students in Hamilton were arrested first, in very orderly fashion. With high city officials and civil rights personalities watching, the police were unusually sensitive to any potential charges of brutality, and there were no incidents. But then the police moved on to the other buildings. Cops are usually paid to put down riots. That night at Columbia, it was the cops who rioted. They dragged out unresisting demonstrators, beating them as they went. They threw around furniture and beat bystanders and reporters. The action lasted three hours. At the end, 720 had been arrested, and hundreds injured.

The next day, sociologist Kenneth Clark and City Human Rights Commissioner William Booth wrote an open letter to the police. They had witnessed the whole affair and had nothing but praise for the police handling of the blacks. As for the whites, it was another story altogether. They told how, after the demonstrators had been removed from one building, they could see through a window cops ripping up a room, throwing furniture and books around, breaking chairs, etc. This story should be remembered along with Grayson Kirk's question the next day as he surveyed the wreckage of his office: "What kind of people could do such a thing?"

What kind of people could be concerned with damage to *property* that day? During the night hundreds of students had to be treated by doctors; many were sent to the hospital.

Many bystanders, including a professor, were led from the campus, injured and sobbing. Columbia's rabbi was carried out bleeding and unconscious. Most students hadn't fought back; the violence was gratuitous. A young doctor who came on campus to treat the injured said: "I saw one policeman simply yank a young man's legs apart and deliberately kick him right in the groin."

All during the occupation, the administration, loyally supported by the daily press, had maintained that the occupation was the work of a "tiny minority" of "extremists." In reality, not only were there perhaps a thousand students in the buildings, but additional hundreds were directly involved in supporting activities. Hundreds more were in the green-armband brigade of sympathetic peacekeepers. Beyond that, perhaps thousands supported some or all of the demands of the occupiers. The support brought together a wide variety of student leaders and student organizations, including the president and vice-president of the university student council and the president of the senior class, who, along with a long list of others, signed a statement supporting the full list of demands, including amnesty. Still, it *was* only a minority, however large, who had *actively* backed the occupation.

The bust changed all that. Tuesday morning, the Columbia *Spectator* expressed the feelings of the majority of the students on the Morningside Heights campus: in place of an editorial it had a large empty space, surrounded by a black border. Tuesday was a day of shock, as hundreds came home from the courthouse to nurse their wounds. But shock turned to fury, against the police, against the trustees, and above all against Grayson Kirk and David Truman. The call for a general strike against the university was renewed. After a few days of discussion, the strike leaders decided that any group of 70 people—students or non-students—could send a delegate to the newly enlarged Strike Coordinating Committee. The Coordinating Committee proceeded to declare that attendance at classes or meetings with professors in university academic buildings was strike-breaking. By the end of the week, eighty per cent of the students in the undergraduate college were on strike, along with many others in other schools of the university. More than 6,000 students as well as several hundred community people, high-school students and university employees, were represented on the Strike Coordinating Committee.

This was a great victory for the Left. It was not only that SDS was leading large numbers of students in a sustained and serious struggle, but that large numbers of students were taking the initiative themselves. Throughout the university, in every school and department, students were demanding radical changes in Columbia's educational system. Thousands of students sent their representatives off to the Coordinating Committee with mandates to stick to the original six points. Students who had never thought much about Vietnam before were denouncing IDA. Students who had worked for McCarthy were talking about revolution.

Growing practically overnight from a tight-knit minority to the largest student organization in the university isn't easy, however, and the Strike Coordinating Committee soon began to show signs of strain. It represented students whose political awakening came the night of the bust, as well as SDS veterans of years of radical struggle. There were students who had been outraged by the police brutality and students who were still wearing bandages. There were students whose resentment against years of impersonal lectures and childish dorm regulations surfaced for the first time during the occupation. And there were militants who wouldn't have been at all sorry to see the community people come and burn the place down.

For the liberal and less politically militant students, the police invasion was the central issue. (The police continued to occupy the campus for days.) Cops were a much more visible feature of Columbia's deterioration than "imperialism," and cops, at least, could be removed. "Cops must go," said their leaflets. "A free university necessitates an open society." Kirk and Truman were other obvious obstacles to reform, so Kirk and Truman had to go along with their police force. But for the veterans of the occupation, the cops and the administrators were only the symbols, not the source of Columbia's sickness. "The cops are not the issue," their leaflets insisted. The cops had done no more than make people realize that "violence is what this university is about." IDA and the gym, racism and the war, were still the issues.

The deepest division was over what should become of the university itself. The more liberal, less radical students believed that the university could be "restructured" through administrative and procedural changes, into a democratic community of students and faculty. What had happened, they thought, was that the university administration had lost touch with the students and community people. If students had something to say about discipline, curriculum, the grading system, IDA, and Columbia's real estate, the university could function smoothly and avoid repeated breakdowns. What the Coordinating Committee had to do, then, was to buckle down to the business of reforming the university.

Now the more radical students, SDS'ers, and most building occupiers had long since lost interest in getting a piece of the power. No doubt the university could eventually be reformed so that the students could help run it—but who wanted to help run it? The university was as much a part of the undemocratic, capitalist system as the army. In fact, its function was complementary to the army's. Columbia could no more go clean and stop being an accomplice in imperialism than it could give up its fat corporate donations and military contracts. It would never be any more just, democratic, and truthful than the society it served. So long before you start thinking about how you are going to run the university, you had better think about where you are going to go with it, and how far you can get with it in this society.

The division proved to be insurmountable. Understandably enough, the liberals were impatient to do something constructive about making Columbia livable. What the radicals were saying seemed obstructive, vindictive, or just plain irrelevant. Of course, to the radicals, the "restructuring" line was equally irrelevant. Maybe in March they would have bitten, but a lot had happened since March. Now they were no more interested in restructuring the university than they were in restructuring the Pentagon. They were interested in radically changing the whole society. They had no easy answers for the less radical students, only a long, hard struggle to offer. In mid-May the Coordinating Committee split, with the moderates going off to form the Students for a Restructured University (SRU). The SRU remained true to the original six points but was largely devoted to studying plans for reforming the university. The Strike Coordinating Committee continued to concentrate on extramural issues.

All of these divisions complicated the history of the next few weeks. But the main fact about the remainder of the school year is that Columbia College stayed closed. The Strike Coordinating Committee, in a measure, took over the educational functions of the university. It urged faculty members and others who supported the strike to set up "liberated classes." Almost anything could be considered a liberated class (as opposed to scabbing) as long as it wasn't held in university buildings and as long as it was run democratically. Many of these classes were merely continuations of pre-strike classes. In others, the same old people showed up but chose to discuss a new subject. Some classes were entirely new: Marxist Economics, the New Journalism, etc. Meanwhile the Coordinating Committee held meetings to explain the history and background of the strike, and sponsored speakers on such topics as "Imperialism in Latin America," "A Radical Critique of Traditional Historiography," and "The Alliance of the Alienated—Women, Blacks, Youth."

The liberated classes were soon so routine that it was hard to remember what university buildings had ever been used for. Confrontations were far from over, however. For one thing, the campus was still conquered territory as far as the police were concerned. On May 8, a band of demonstrators, demanding an open campus, sat-in in front of the police lines. Later that week, a committee set up to investigate the disorder invited the Strike Coordinating Committee to send representatives to testify. They came, but their testimony consisted entirely of readings from an article by Vice-President David Truman—on the use of fact-finding committees as a mechanism to quell dissent! This was about as much of a dialogue with the faculty and administration as the Coordinating Committee got into. The Committee also steered clear of factional fights with the break-away SRU. There were more important things to do.

Instead, the Coordinating Committee directed its attention to new offensives against the university in its role in the society. One of Columbia's real estate practices was to buy up old apartment buildings and allow them to deteriorate

until the tenants were forced to move out. Then the buildings could be demolished and the land put to more profitable
uses. Right near the university was one such Columbia-
owned building in an advanced stage of neglect. In winter it
had no heat. The locks on the doors were broken, but went
unrepaired, as did the leaks in the ceiling and the broken
plumbing. Trash was allowed to pile up in the basement and
there were numerous other fire and health hazards. On May
17, fifty residents of the community occupied the building,
while a thousand students and community people demonstrated in support outside. The police came and arrested 140
of the occupiers and demonstrators.

Three days later, the Dean summoned four leaders of the
original occupation to appear before him. The students
were already facing criminal charges for trespassing and
other crimes, so the Dean's action seemed to be putting
them in double jeopardy. Whatever the legalistic fine points,
the campus was tense enough so that the summons looked like
an open provocation. If a confrontation was what the administration wanted, plenty of students were in the mood to
oblige. The four students refused to attend the hearing. That
didn't stop the Dean, though; the four were suspended for
not appearing. A crowd rallying to support the four marched
into Hamilton Hall to protest to the Dean. Apparently the
rally was planned as just that—a protest, and no more. But
Dean Coleman remembered what had happened the last
time students had marched into Hamilton. He quickly issued
an ultimatum that the students were to leave within ten minutes. There is only one response to that kind of order. Once
again, students found themselves sitting down in Hamilton.
As the news got around campus, hundreds of students
rushed to Hamilton, till there were two thousand outside
and four hundred sitting-in. Coleman again warned that if

they weren't out within ten minutes the police would be called, and that anyone arrested in the building would automatically be suspended.

Everyone had known that a second round had to follow the bloody bust of May 1. Even if the administration had been conciliatory, it probably couldn't have pacified the students in the two short weeks since the bust. But the administration hadn't made the slightest gesture of conciliation. While the lawns of the campus were covered with striking students, the administration reiterated its determination to crush the small band of terrorists. On May 13, as Congress was muttering about cutting off federal scholarship and loan money to disruptive students, Grayson Kirk summed up his experience:

> During the last three weeks, the faculty, the administrative officers, and most of the students of Columbia University have been engaged in a *struggle to preserve academic freedom . . . against a small minority's* effort to halt the basic operations of the university. . . . We have therefore resisted a natural temptation to imitate the tactics of those who are bent on destroying the principles and the practices by which a university must live. (Emphasis added.)

And now, as students were once again filling Hamilton, the administration got ready to use *its* favorite tactic—the police.

After Coleman's warning, students who were already facing criminal charges left the building to avoid second arrests. Their places were taken by new people, and the second occupation of Hamilton got under way. Early that morning the police came through the tunnels which connect many of the buildings on campus and peacefully removed the occupiers. Outside, on the campus, four or five thousand students had gathered, and stood watching the police massing on the streets around Columbia. Screaming "Keep off our campus!"

to the police, they barricaded the main entrances to the campus. The police in Hamilton were forced to retreat back through the tunnels.

Fearing that the students might recapture Columbia, the administration asked the police to come in and clear the campus. The police didn't need much of an invitation. Hundreds of helmeted riot police streamed in through the side entrances. Others charged through the barricades. Once inside, the police outdid their first performance. A leader of SAS was clubbed to the ground and then kicked systematically by a crowd of cops. They forced one set of students into a corner where they proceeded to beat them repeatedly. Having ordered all students to get off the campus or to get into their dorm rooms, they followed them into one dorm with drawn guns, beating everyone in sight.

This time passive resistance was out of the question. Bands of students dashed around the campus, in and out of the buildings. From inside the dorms, they attacked the cops with showers of bottles and ashtrays. One group rolled a tree-sized flower pot to the edge of a roof and pushed it off so that it crushed a police car below. When an ambulance could not get in through the great iron gates to the campus, which the police had locked, the students ripped the gate down.

There was, essentially, no rest of the school year at Columbia. The school was closed. Commencement had to be held indoors, virtually behind locked doors. Kirk could not speak at the ceremony for fear of disruption. Many people attended a counter-commencement held by the SRU, and others walked out of the official one. After graduation, most students finally left. A large core remained at Columbia to run a "liberation school." Throughout the summer, this liberation school was the chief focus of radical action in New York, and a place for research and discussion and planning for the year to come.

On August 23, Grayson Kirk resigned as president of Columbia. No gesture of conciliation was intended. The next day the trustees appointed as acting president a figure well known to student radicals—Andrew Cordier, head of Columbia's School of International Relations, the scene of many of Columbia's studies in support of the empire and the recipient of CIA grants to perform secret research. Cordier's past was even shadier. As a high official in the United Nations' Congo mission in 1960, it was Cordier, more than anyone else, who maneuvered the downfall of the popular elected premier, Patrice Lumumba. Cordier helped bolster the power of leaders more friendly to the United States and took steps that indirectly assured Lumumba's murder. Apparently the trustees felt that all Columbia needed was a reliable counter-insurgency expert at the helm. Everything that SDS had been saying about the links between imperialism, racism, and Columbia University, was neatly summed up by Cordier's appointment.

* * *

If the American movement had given up and dissolved in June, Columbia would have provided a fitting finale. At Columbia in April everything came together—all of the issues and many of the people out of the last five years. There was the struggle against racism, which began with students leaving school to go to little towns in the South to register people to vote. Now that struggle had come home to the university. There was the struggle against the war, which began in the

university with teach-ins and then went out to the streets and
the neighborhoods. Now it had come back to the university.
(In fact the first time we, the authors, entered the Columbia campus was in the spring of 1965, going to an Independent Committee on Vietnam meeting, to argue for taking the
anti-war movement off the campus and into the community.
The argument was so popular that we didn't really come back
until three years later, to join the demonstration outside
Hamilton Hall.)

For both issues, the university was no longer just the base
of operations; it was the target. All over the country for three
years, students had slowly been following the trail they
started on in 1964 or 1965, tracing racism and imperialism
back to their sources. By the spring of 1968, one of the places
the trail had led to was the university. What happened at Columbia could have happened, and almost did, at any of a number of universities. If things came together faster at Columbia, maybe it was because they were closer there to start with.
Harlem is just outside the gate, and New York has been a center of anti-war sentiment from the start.

Even the people came together at Columbia. There was
Tom Hayden, a founder of SDS and a pioneer in community
organizing. There were the intelligence experts of the North
American Congress on Latin America, who uncovered a lot
of the dirt on IDA and Columbia's real estate holdings. There
were liberal blacks from the NAACP who simply opposed
the gym and there were SNCC leaders who opposed the system. There were black nationalists from Harlem, in brilliant dashikis. There were reporters from Liberation News
Service and the underground press, who came to watch and
stayed to sit-in. There were harried-looking professors who
had once starred in teach-ins, serene-faced hippies up from

the Lower East Side, and, of course, the cops, some of them
even beginning to look a little familiar after so many demonstrations.

But Columbia wasn't a finale; it was a kind of graduation.
All through the movement, except for a short spree at Berkeley, radical students had been fighting for someone else—
black people, Vietnamese, Mexican grape pickers, or Puerto
Rican welfare mothers. Students were missionairies. They
joined the Peace Corps to save the Bolivians or they joined
SNCC to organize the Alabamans. Somewhere along the line
this began to change. Bleeding hearts began to change into
bloody heads. After a summer in Mississippi, it was hard to
file back, IBM cards in hand, for fall registration. After scuf-
fling with cops at a demonstration, it was hard to sit still
while an (unarmed) professor rapped on about the merits
of our pluralistic system. As the war dragged on, consuming
more and more working-class kids, things changed even
faster. We discovered that students weren't the precious natural resource we had thought they were. They could be
drafted. If you slipped in your studies or irritated a dean,
you could be suspended—from school to Vietnam. The idea
of the university as a community of scholars began to pall very
fast after the administration added the death sentence to its
repertory of disciplinary measures.

At Columbia, students began to take up the struggles
against the war and racism as their own fight. The issues were
still, at first, Vietnam and racism, but the battlefield was
the university. As the struggle grew, it became a struggle *for*
the university. When the police recaptured it, we had our
hardest lesson yet: The system didn't mind cracking the
skulls it had spent so much money to stuff with knowledge.
There was no public outcry when Columbia University decided that damage to property was a more serious matter than

damage to one batch of students. In fact, the newspapers lied about the causes, winked, and went on to applaud the restoration of law and order. Students could be beaten, jailed, shot, shoved around, lied about, just like black people, Vietnamese, Mexican grape pickers, etc. After all, America has plenty of students to spare.

Columbia may have done more for race relations than all the thousands of dollars that middle-class white liberals ever poured into SNCC. For once, white students were fighting for their own thing, not a few steps ahead, not safely behind, but right there beside black people. True, the black students remained aloof in their building. But after the first night, the white students stopped feeling left out; they had their own problems. Many white radicals had been getting a little tired of the morally satisfying but ultimately vicarious job of "supporting our black brothers," anyway. In what sense were they "our black brothers" until white students began to get a little black themselves? If there was any doubt on that score, the U.S. Army and the New York police settled it. For purposes of law enforcement, in New York or Vietnam, "students are niggers."

Except in the trivial sense of cheering for the same team or wearing the same color ties, students have never had much of a feeling of collective identity in this country. Columbia produced a real surge of student consciousness. The Columbia students discovered that students were some kind of a group, not a class and not a race (whatever the police think), but a group just the same. Radical students had gone a long way to avoid this discovery—to Mississippi for the summer, to Washington for the annual marches—but there it was; they were students at a university. It was important to learn this, because the enemy wasn't any longer tucked safely away in the Pentagon, or the White House, or Wall Street. He, or his friends, were right here at the university. When you see what he does in Harlem or in Southeast Asia, you begin to wonder what he's doing to you, and what's in it for him.

There's a funny thing about feeling the full depth of this kind of student consciousness: as soon as you grasp it, it's practically useless. When someone finds out what it means to be a Negro, he doesn't get any lighter for it. When a worker gains class-consciousness, he doesn't automatically retire or get promoted to foreman. But when a student finds out what it means in this society to be a student at a university, the game is already up. He isn't interested in being a student anymore, or in being any of the things students are supposed to be. The star graduates of the Math Commune or Low Library heard their last lecture on April 22.

Something happened to the idea of the university itself in the process. It's one thing to know that the university president is a real estate dealer; it's something else to know that the university itself is a bunch of buildings. The university as academic community was practically unassailable, but the university as buildings could be seized and occupied. Buildings are property, and as the police demonstrated, property is more important than life, truth, justice, or any of the other things that universities are supposed to be about. The people who learned that at Columbia learned everything that the university was ever going to teach them.

CHAPTER EIGHT

Graduation

The student movement is part of the whole people's movement. The upsurge of the student movement will inevitably promote an upsurge of the whole people's movement.

—Mao Tse-tung

Create two, three, many Columbias!
—Columbia Strike Committee

We have seen a little of how radical student movements developed in the United States and a few European countries. Movements have grown out of the universities of many other countries over the last few years. How is it that universities have generated radical movements in countries as disparate as Germany and Uruguay, the United States and Japan, or Sweden and Mexico? Universities are certainly not supposed to produce revolutionaries. The reasons they do, we think, go back to their functions in capitalist societies and to their peculiarities as social systems composed almost entirely of young people.

* * *

For a moment, consider the university simply as a place where people live, or at least spend most of their time. It's a place where large numbers of young people are crowded

159

together to wait out the gap between childhood and man-
or womanhood, a gap of somewhere between four and nine
years, depending on the degree of manhood one aspires to.
For reasons of its own, advanced industrial society increasingly requires a long stint of vocational rehabilitation between the mindlessness of high school and the privilege of
working.

Adolescence wasn't always an embarrassing sort of larval
stage. There were times and there are still places where
youths are accepted as full-fledged people at the age of thir-
teen or so. Not all societies can afford to waste a chunk of
people's most productive years by putting them away to incu-
bate in isolated campuses. But in the countries we have
been talking about, many people get to be seventeen or eighteen without ever once questioning the fact that they're supposed to be helpless, ignorant, and useless for at least four
more years. If you are told over and over by serious grown-
ups that you are helpless, ignorant, and useless, sure enough,
you start shuffling your feet and acting that way. Especially
when you're penned in with thousands of other students doing the exact same thing. Like inmates in a sanitarium, students talk half wistfully, half fearfully, about the "real world"
and what they'll do there when they're finally deemed
"ready" to leave.

The other side of the university as detention camp is, of
course, the university as playground. In America especially,
there's no getting around it, many universities are very nice
places to live. The company is good, and it's a good deal more
indulgent of deviations than the company you'll find in most
institutions. Then the hours are good—you can set your
own work-pace within pretty wide limits. Since students are
usually unemployed or close to it, a good deal of shiftlessness
and irresponsibility is practically expected of them. Many re-

actionaries have correctly perceived that one reason for student demonstrations is that students have the time to demonstrate.

Still, students continue to take vacations from universities, not to them. Universities are after all very peculiar kinds of communities. Although the population is overwhelmingly students, it's not students who make the rules. Take the rules concerning sex. Almost all students are well past puberty, yet universities insist on sexual abstinence. Strange taboos surround the meetings of the sexes: lights on at all times, door one foot ajar, not after ten P.M., etc. Many universities do encourage their students to find a suitable mate on the premises, so long as the relationship develops in the clear light of public lounges, pizza stands, and football stadiums. Anyone who sneaks a little premarital intimacy can expect to feel the full weight of academic vindictiveness. For instance, a few weeks before the Columbia uprising, a girl was suspended from Barnard (the women's college associated with Columbia) for surreptitiously living off campus with her boyfriend. (They later lived together more openly in an occupied building.) Students are free, but not free to do very much.

Of course universities are not just places to live. It is the business of universities to sort out their students into categories useful to real-world employers: "good" (start at $8000), "fair" (start at $6500), and "reject" (don't start). The sorting is done largely through the mechanism of exams. If exams did nothing more than determine your whole future, they would be bad enough. The real horror of exams is that they can also ruin your life as a student. One big difference between students and the university's paid employees is that the latter often have some degree of job security. Every exam brings home to students how tenuous their stay at the

university is. The first few failures bring only mild igno-
miny, humiliation, etc., but a long enough list of failures is
a one-way ticket straight into the working force (or in the
United States, straight to Vietnam). Adults may treat pre-
exam suffering along with acne as one of the humorous features of adolescence, but there's nothing funny about it.
Every year, suicides and nervous breakdowns testify to the
brutality of the students' situation and, of course, to the
toughness of those who get through.

If you take a hard look at what are supposed to be "the
best years of your life," you can only wonder why massive
student rebellions didn't occur sooner than they did. Actually, students were quietly, unconsciously, developing styles
of resistance well before it ever occurred to anyone to break
up an exam, or occupy a building. Teachers probably no-
ticed this before students themselves were aware of it. A radical teacher at UCLA wrote:

> Some students . . . are expert con artists who know perfectly
> well what's happening. They want the degree or the 2-S and
> spend their years on the old plantation alternately laughing
> and cursing as they play the game. If their egos are strong, they
> cheat a lot. And, of course, even the Toms are angry deep down
> somewhere. But it comes out in passive rather than active ag-
> gression. They're unexplainably thick-witted and subject to
> frequent spells of laziness. They misread simple questions.
> They spend their nights mechanically outlining history chap-
> ters and meticulously failing to comprehend a word of what's
> in front of them. (Jerry Farber, in *The Student as Nigger*.)

In the mid-sixties student resistance entered a new phase—
the cultural revolution. Probably if any group is left alone
long enough, excluded from the bulk of society, it begins to
shape a culture of its own. Young people are isolated only
temporarily, but the isolation can be profound. For most
people who go to college, which is more people every year,

the years from around seventeen to twenty-one or even older are spent almost entirely with other young people—eating, sleeping, playing, studying. Contacts with adults, who are likely to be parents, professors, or cops, are usually involuntary and uncomfortable.

No one is exactly sure how or when youth became conscious of being an out-group and began to assemble its own culture. From the blacks they took rock music, pot, and a whole new vocabulary unknown to white adults. From the white lower class, they picked up smatterings of motorcycle culture. From the white ex-middle-class Bohemians, they borrowed bits of Eastern mysticism and pop art faddery. Somehow all these things began to come together into a culture strong enough to stand on its own as an alternative way of living.

In 1965 Bob Dylan cut loose from the folk sounds favored at the Newport Festival and sang, "How does it feel to be on your own, with no direction home, a complete unknown, like a rolling stone?" Kids started finding out. In the summer of 1967 a trickle of drop-outs began to flow out of suburban towns and campuses to New York and San Francisco. 1967 was the summer of the Great Walk-out, when tens of thousands of kids converged to form city-sized communities of their own. The same thing began to happen on a smaller scale in Europe. Migrant youths traveled to Paris, Munich, Florence, or London, moving in the new underground of escaped students.

What the universities lost in terms of population was barely significant. Of all the students who developed shoulder-length hair and grooved on rock or acid, very few took the big step out of academia. But what the university lost by way of credibility may never be entirely recouped. Youth culture is the antithesis of university culture and the "culture" universities market. What universities extolled as discipline, youth culture mocked as a "bag." What universities prize as "honor" is just the ability to act as if knowledge were private property. Why shouldn't students work communally, sharing what they know as well as the things they have? The university's attitude toward sex was too perverted to discuss. Did they expect students to spend four years masturbating in their library cubicles? Even the substance of university culture was highly questionable—all too verbal and linear and orderly to have anything much to do with how things are. Finally, the university's ultimate justification as preparation for the "real world" was debunked as the real world's ontological status slid to "unreal," "plastic," a "bad trip."

The youth cultural revolt always had an overt political cast. It went without saying that hippies were anticapitalist and anti-authoritarian. A few groups even bothered to say it. The Diggers in San Francisco practiced socialism by stealing food to give away. There are the Yippies (Youth International Party) who unleashed the depravity of the Democratic Party at its 1968 convention. New York has a small but mobile group called "Up Against the Wall, Motherfuckers" whose manifesto declares that "the future of our movement is the future of crime in the streets." In Europe, provos and Situationists harassed the bourgeoisie with practical jokes and equally impractical demands. There's a lot to that reactionary intuition that lumps together hippies, students, and radical "terrorists."

Very few students ever joined a commune or became socialists because of the prevailing youth culture. The real impact of the youth revolt was neither organizational nor ideological. What was happening was a Marcusean psycho-dimensional breakthrough: being "in" or "out" of a closed world of degrees, salaries, and credit cards stopped being the interesting modalities. Things were up, or down, or they were out-of-sight. Imagination crashed through the billboard-textbook definitions of things and demanded new words or new sounds. Maybe it would be nice to know everything the professor knows, but you wouldn't want to be him.

For a couple of years, all this was building up quietly inside otherwise docile minds. If you couldn't do anything about things, you could at least resist in your imagination. But fantasy is the substratum of reality. When you can dream of locking up the tight-lipped, grey-flanneled dean in his own little dean's office, when you can imagine hanging red and black flags from every window of the Sorbonne, you are halfway to doing it. Youth culture, which started out as a technique for surviving bad trips like school, was the springboard to open rebellion.

* * *

Universities are not just peculiar social systems. They are not endowed, staffed and accredited for the single purpose of repressing young people. They do many things depending on what society demands of them. Over the years, the demands have changed and universities have changed to meet them. Understanding what's happening to the schools is the key to understanding what's going on with their students. The stresses of institutions emerge in history as the tensions of people.

The old universities of the Western world did one thing and did it well: they produced, and reproduced, the elite. At Cambridge and at Oxford, at the Sorbonne and at Florence, the sons of aristocrats, academicians, and high-level businessmen and government officials were trained to be aristocrats and academicians, high-level businessmen and government officials. The training really had two parts. On the one hand universities were the home of humanism. They had to instil an unspecialized set of attitudes associated with the liberal arts, classics, philosophy, and art. Good breeding required both humanist tastes and the manners of a successful courtier. On the other hand, universities were the home of critical reason. They trained people in the specialized knowledge of the time and served as centers of scholarship. There were many gentlemanly professions—history, linguistics, law, science. And there were many leisured gentlemen who learned these things for pleasure. Many eminent nineteenth-century scientists were little more than avid hobbyists. At the time no one would have described the university as having two sides: one to do with specialized knowledge and one to do with upper-class attitudes. The two were inseparable. The humanist values made a man a gentleman and only a gentleman was privileged to glimpse the recondite knowledge stored in the university.

The old, elite type of university offered a highly individualized, custom-fitted style of education. Recall that even before there were buildings and academic hierarchies called universities, aristocratic young men would get together and hire some scholars to instruct them. With the institutionalization of higher education into universities, the relation between scholars and students changed very little. Students still represented the tiny upper class that paid for the universities, and the universities existed to render a service to their students. At places like Oxford and Cambridge, private tutorials, independent studies, and other personalized programs introduced the young man to an aristocratic approach to learning as well as to whatever substantive knowledge he might require for a gentlemanly career. Residence halls, student unions, debating societies, etc., familiarized him with the people and the mores of his own class.

The industrial revolution at first placed no revolutionary demands on universities. Of course, greater emphasis would have to be put on the actual teaching mission of universities (as opposed to their ideological role) and especially on the technical subjects. Under the reorganization plan of Wilhelm von Humboldt, the German universities adjusted rather gracefully. Humboldt's plan emphasized research and specialization, for which the graduate and professional schools were developed. A loose curriculum was formulated, and elective courses were distinguished from required ones. As the reorganized universities began to produce class after class of first-rate scholars and scientists, German industry picked up steam and overtook England's in a number of key fields.

The German reorganization was eventually adopted, whole or piecemeal, by universities in other industrializing countries. It had little impact, though, on the university as a community. Streamlining the university did not yet mean channeling the students. If the universities produced more than the aristocracy, they did not have to produce *much* more. Industry needed only a small technically trained elite, not masses of skilled manpower. In rapidly industrializing countries, like England, Germany and the United States, as the upper class came to include the industrial rich, there were always enough upper-class youths to fill the new technical elite as well as the more traditional gentlemanly professions. Like its feudal ancestor, the nineteenth-century university was supported by the upper class to reproduce the upper class.

Things have changed. Industry can no longer get by with a Kelvin or a Maxwell as a consultant and a few hundred illiterates on the assembly line. Instead of relying on the vagaries

of a couple of academic researchers, industries hire whole
regiments of PhD's to churn out the innovations and divisions of engineers and technicians to put the innovations
into production. The bigger the industry, the more it requires additional forces of economists, sociologists, psychologists, and lawyers to keep things running smoothly. The
defense industries, public and private, are adding more and
more mathematicians, linguists, political scientists, even an-
thropologists, to their payrolls. What big industry can't use,
big government can employ as planners and analysts. Back
on the assembly line, high-school graduates are filling the
jobs once held down by eleven-year-olds. Armies of college-
educated teachers are required to produce all the white collar, skilled, and semi-skilled workers.

What this means for the university is that the old trickle
of hand-crafted scholars won't do; masses of graduates are
needed, each one tailored and labeled for one of the masses
of government or industrial slots. In most countries, universities have responded more than adequately, at least as
far as volume of students goes. In the U.S., which reached the
stage of needing masses of college-educated manpower soon-
est, the number of students in all kinds of colleges and universities increased from about 1.4 million before World War
II to 2.7 million in 1955 and almost 7.0 million in 1968. In
Europe, the changes occurred slightly later, but, for example,
in France, enrollment went from 304,000 to 491,000 in four
years, from 1960 to 1964.

Few kinds of communities can undergo a severalfold increase in population without profound qualitative changes.
Universities were no exception. Advanced industrialization
certainly brought a measure of affluence and democratiza-
tion of opportunity, but it did not mean that every student

was a member or a potential member of the corporate-government elite. Although the universities are still financed and controlled by this elite, they no longer function simply to reproduce it. Universities accept all kinds of people and produce all kinds of people. Some students, notable for special intelligence, ambition, or social connections, graduate directly into the upper ranks of business and government. Some students, less lucky or more stolid, are diverted into long years of specialized training to become the super-technicians—scientists, engineers, economists, or academicians. Others are brushed over with a thin veneer of liberal arts and tossed out on the job markets to become grade-school teachers or low-level administrators. Still others are weeded out early and slide down into the sub-professions. In sum, the university takes a heterogeneous group of freshmen, turns them into a homogeneous mass of students, and then, in the course of four years, differentiates them into a heterogeneous array of leaders and followers, managers and managed.

Of course, not all universities produce every variety of graduate. There has been a degree of specialization of the universities themselves. England is an extreme example, where Oxford and Cambridge retain in large measure their ancient role of socializing the aristocracy, while training in technical skills is relegated to the new universities, the polytechnical schools, and other colleges. In France, a handful of Grandes Écoles continues to produce the leaders of government and industry. Less widely known, but abundantly documented (see Mills' *The Power Elite* and Domhoff's *Who Rules America?*), is the fact that a disproportionate number of American government and corporate leaders come from Harvard, Princeton, and Yale. The universities we have talked about, however—the Sorbonne, Rome, Turin, Frankfurt, Berlin, and (to a lesser extent) Columbia—are relatively unspecialized, contributing to the elite, the drop-outs, and every variety of worker in between.

In the most advanced countries, universities have acquired an additional function that has little to do with the business of producing graduates. Technical information has become an important enough commodity to warrant an industry of its own, the "knowledge industry," and the university is a key unit of production. University labs turn out the basic research which underlies applied industrial research, as well as much applied research. In 1964 universities spent two billion dollars for research, about ten per cent of the total national expenditures on research and development. Universities perform some research in their own laboratories. They directly operate some government research facilities, such as Brookhaven National Laboratories, and front for others, such as IDA. Then there are countless informal ways that universities help out. Professors moonlight as consultants for government and industry; executives go back to school to keep up with technology, and so on. It's no accident that the great centers of technologically advanced industries are in locations near the great technological universities. (For instance, Route 128 around Boston links many electronics and aerospace industries to nearby MIT and Harvard.)

The function of the university has changed in all advanced industrial countries, but few countries have adapted their universities' structure to meet their altered function. Most European universities don't even meet the entrance requirements to the twentieth century. The student body multiplied many times over in the last fifty years, but few new classrooms were built, and fewer still of the laboratories, language labs, television-equipped lecture rooms, etc. that are the physical counterparts of the new mass training function of the university. Scholarships and loans are so scarce that few of the new "mass" base of the university can afford to attend school full time. If they did attend, there would be no room in lecture halls or libraries. Even if there were no problem of where to sit in class, there is the problem of where to sleep at night. Dormitories are scarcer on the continent than motels. So most students read the professor's lectures after work and show up once a year for exams. Whether you go to class or not, the education is likely to be hopelessly dull and anachronistic.

This situation is intolerable both to the students and to industry and government. Students go to universities expecting two things: First they'd like a glimpse of the traditional university aura: humanism, liberal arts, critical reason, etc. Second, they'd like to learn whatever skills are necessary for a job, preferably a job which will pay well enough so that they can occasionally indulge in the other interests they acquire at the university. In most European universities, students lose on both counts. The mass, dictatorial teaching of the liberal arts turns out to be not just a low-grade version of a liberal arts education, but a perversion of it. As for the practical side of education, out-of-date medicine or engineering isn't even partial training, it's useless. Many students started pressuring for university reforms years ago. They wanted modern curricula and teaching methods, adequate physical facilities, and a little more personal attention. They wanted to be trained for a job, educated for a lifetime, and treated like human beings in the process.

Meanwhile, business and government officials had a competing demand for reforms. They weren't concerned that universities are overcrowded, understaffed, and consequently more impersonal every year, or that the philosophy professor was deaf and the sociology professor gave multiple choice tests. They were concerned about "cost-effectiveness"—more scholars for the dollar. The obvious strategy for increasing the productive capacity of universities was to speed up the production line. In France, Germany, and Italy the tactics which have been proposed invariably include limiting the amount of time students can stay at the university, imposing earlier channeling into a specialty through curriculum requirements, and eliminating liberal arts "frills" wherever possible. Physicists don't need to study art history any more than government bureaucrats need to study astronomy.

Needless to say, the official reforms were not exactly what students had in mind. Certainly they wanted to be able to get jobs when they got out. And maybe the university was becoming such a bore that people wouldn't mind seeing a couple of semesters knocked off their student lifetimes. Maybe the liberal arts courses weren't worth taking anyway, if you could stand the other courses. But the official reforms excluded the possibility of ever having any reforms that were real, as the students saw them. With every official shake-up for efficiency, the university regressed a little further from any semblance of a "community of scholars."

The official reforms provided one of the bitterest lessons of European post-war student experience. They made it quite clear that the interests of students are one thing and the interests of government and business are another. While students looked to the university for knowledge, for community; government looked to it for manpower. While students saw themselves as the subjects of the educational process, government saw them as the objects of educational processing. In fact, if the government could have done it, it would have by-passed the university and tried to reform the students directly.

It's a hard thing to set out on a stroll through a museum and wake up on a factory conveyor belt. Maybe it wouldn't have led to a blow-up if students could have found some other grounds on which to identify with the men who control universities. But there was no evidence that most students had any interests in common with the men who controlled the universities. First, the students are not, by and large, in the same class as the education moguls. As the student body had expanded, it expanded way beyond the sons of the elite, but the group of men who finance and control universities remained pretty much what it always had been, the government and business elite. It didn't take a whole lot of class consciousness or Marxist theory for students to figure out that the university was an instrument by which one class dominates another. Even that wouldn't have been so bad, however, if it hadn't been for Vietnam. However distantly, every European government seemed to be in collusion with the United States. Vietnam showed what capitalism is all about, once you get beneath the layer of rhetoric about "democracy" and "progress." If that was what it was about, then it wasn't something that you submitted to being hammered into shape to serve. It might be endurable to be a cog in a tractor, but who wants to be a cog in a tank?

* * *

In the United States, the situation is very different. American universities may have their faults, but you can hardly accuse them of not doing what they are supposed to do. Compared to their European counterparts, American universities and colleges are rational, efficient institutions, neatly adapted to the needs of the expanding economy, industry, and empire. (In fact, the reforms mapped out for the European universities are, in large part, attempts to imitate the American model.)

The first American universities were designed to resemble the European universities, but, of course, the feudal social heritage couldn't be built in. America's real break with the European university style came with the Civil War and the establishment of the land grant colleges. The West was a clean slate. The new land grant schools were set up to serve their communities: to train people in modern agriculture or mining, to do research for local industry, to educate local youngsters, rich or poor. Today the spirit of the pastoral little land grant schools pervades almost all American universities. If the student body trebles, or if the "community" develops an interest in nuclear fission or counter-insurgency techniques, the university complies readily. Their basic mission is to serve.

Probably there have never been truly autonomous universities anywhere. But the European universities have managed out of sheer inertia to preserve at least an illusion of autonomy, even if all it means is an unhealthy divorce from the needs of the general society. American universities never aspired to autonomy. As training grounds, as advisory centers, as business partners, American universities are as thoroughly integrated into American society as our military academies. In fact, American universities can hardly even be said to have problems of their own. Conflicts within our universities don't reflect trouble between the university and the society, they reflect conflicts within the society itself.

American universities are, on the face of it, more stable than their European counterparts, by virtue of their fantastic symbiosis with government and industry. But it is the very smoothness of the university's integration that gets it into trouble. If you question the one, you are questioning the other. To challenge IDA is to threaten Columbia University, and to challenge Columbia is to threaten IDA (and all its colleagues). The connections aren't at all theoretical. If you disrupt university classes, you can expect to be threatened by government and business officials, and to be punished by their police. There are no truly "external" issues. A struggle against the war can become a struggle against university complicity and finally a struggle against the university. And, conversely, struggle around an "internal" issue, like student power, escalates almost inevitably into a critique of the whole system.

The American student movement didn't begin as a *students'* movement. People may have had plenty of gripes as students, but these seemed trivial and personal compared to issues like Vietnam, racism, and poverty. (Even the Free Speech Movement at Berkeley was sparked by outside issues— HUAC [the House Un-American Activities Committee] and civil rights.) Vietnam, racism and poverty affect, or at least impinge on, all Americans, not just the ones who happen to be in universities. Yet the movement which has developed around these issues is primarily a student movement. Why— as Dean Rusk must have asked himself everytime he ventured out of Washington—must students be so *sensitive?*

There are the reasons suggested at the beginning of this chapter: students have lots of time and not much responsibility; they read the newspapers; they are physically restless; etc. But you can be all these things and a fascist. They don't explain why students moved to the *left*.

The answer, we think, lies in the university itself. American universities are reliable enough when it comes to job-training, or the production of useful information. But in addition to being a willing handmaid to industry and government, the university remains the repository of Western Civilization: Judeo-Christian ethics, Aristotelian logic, Enlightenment, humanism, etc. In the United States today, these traditions are nothing less than subversive. The hopes of the dead are the harshest indictment of the living. And the modern American multifunctional university never lets you forget it. In Civilization-110 you read the thoughts of Pascal; in Chem-320 you learn how to make napalm. In Econ. you read Samuelson's hymn to American capitalism; in American Lit. you might have to read Dreiser. In Business you cram on real estate laws; in History you skim through Marx. In your spare moments you're encouraged to "keep up" by reading the newspaper.

We shouldn't be surprised when American students become radicals, but when they fail to.

If the liberal arts are intrinsically subversive, why keep them around? Certainly the masses of scientists, technicians, even sociologists would be just as skilled, and probably more tractable, if they had never heard of Socrates. Not all professors can be relied on to teach the liberal arts so tediously as to leave no memory traces in the students' minds. If the liberal arts survive only because of some aging administrator's nostalgia, then it shouldn't be long before American universities undergo their ultimate rationalization to become technical training institutes. But the liberal-arts specialized-training dichotomy is not vestigial. It is deeply rooted in the function of the university and in the needs of capitalism itself.

First, there still is an elite. The ancient function of the university—to train and help perpetuate the tiny corps of men who can run corporations and countries—will be with us as long as the elite is. For these lucky students (whom the university helps select) broad training is still a necessity. The political wisdom and class-consciousness of a Rockefeller are bred as much in the seminar rooms at Harvard as on the tennis courts at Newport.

Second, educators and businessmen increasingly recognize the values of a liberal education for all kinds of people who are way below the power elite. Scientists and engineers are not enough; today's involuted technology requires *creative* scientists and engineers. It isn't out of humanism that MIT makes its freshmen study "humanities." The market is for innovators, "bold, restless, creative" technicians, who will "dare to challenge and dissent." (Read the want ads in *Scientific American*.) Then there are all the new job categories —systems men, programmers, analysts, operations researchers—which proliferate as the knowledge industry expands. Companies like Rand, Simulatrix and their competitors, and the U.S. government pay a lot for these all-purpose troubleshooters, and the only job requirements are a college degree, a quick mind, and no hang-ups. What's developing is a greater and greater need for super-technicians who are both analytically disciplined and imaginative, who can specialize in anything without becoming specialized themselves. Until someone thinks of a better way of producing them, these people will come up through the liberal-arts/technical-training mix that American universities provide.

Still, why should *all* American universities retain this dangerous blend of the liberal arts and the industrial skills? It ought to be possible to set aside one set of schools for the elite (power elite and technical elite) and another for the mass of skilled workers. *De facto,* of course, the universities are partly segregated along these lines. Harvard handles the leadership and Hofstra handles the rank and file. But to push this tendency any further than it's already gone would probably be politically unfeasible—it would be "undemocratic" (whether *that's* a vestigial concept we leave to your judgment). More relevantly, it would also be somewhat dysfunctional. American high schools are a far cry from German *gymnasiums* or French *lycées*. They can't be counted on to weed out the misfits and skim off the cream. Many a poor but bright boy is "discovered" in a low-tuition state school and funneled into corporate leadership. And many a rich dullard is spotted at Harvard and eased into an innocuous career. Although it might be possible to upgrade the high schools into suitable arenas for selection, the present system is far less cumbersome and much more flexible.

There are additional reasons for retaining the liberal arts which have nothing to do with the training of the elite and nothing to do with the demands of technology. Most of the jobs which require a college education are low-level jobs and require no specific knowledge at all. To be a grade-school teacher, a salesman, or a medium-level administrator requires little technical skill, less creativity, and no broad cultural sensitivity. All that's required are the untechnical skills of communicating, organizing material, and coping with a limited range of problems. For education in these general skills, the *content* of education makes very little difference. People can learn to prepare sales brochures by writing term papers on Periclean Athens.

But when you come right down to it, the choice of the liberal arts for content is *not* just arbitrary. To most professors and administrators, the liberal arts ethos corresponds to what they imagine *are* the underlying principles of our "democratic" society. They see nothing dangerous about the liberal arts. On the contrary, the rhetoric of the liberal arts serves to reconcile most students, most of the time, to things-as-they-are. And so long as the liberal arts are taught in an authoritarian fashion (with professors standing at the front of the room, with exams, etc.) they will, for most students, remain rhetoric, to be safely consigned to a tiny corner of the brain. Thus, universities have a crucial ideological function: through the content of their courses, students learn to wield the rhetoric of society, while through the structure of their courses, they learn to deal with the reality of society. In extracurricular activities and in classes, students learn to handle minor responsibility, to function in an organization, to take pride in the system, and to limit their demands on it.

* * *

We've been arguing that advanced capitalist society requires liberal arts training, requires it to be taught along with technical subjects, and in the same multi-purpose universities. It's a calculated risk. The super-rational, well-integrated, multiversity is only as stable as the minds of its students. Every now and then the dikes break and a neatly compartmentalized mind gets blown into a new dimension of revolutionary perspective. Of course hardly anyone becomes seriously unhinged simply by the contrast between Civilization-110 and civilization, or Humanities-220 and humanity. It takes a powerful external stimulus to make the contrast unbearable. For instance, few students can develop more than an academic concern about "war", but tens of thousands will drop their studies to struggle against *the* war in Vietnam. Even at Berkeley in 1964, the students didn't rise up just because it was so degrading to be a student at Berkeley. The substratum of discontent was there, but crises developing from "external" issues set off the struggle.

All universities in authoritarian societies teach conflicting sets of values, and as long as there is a possibility of a
Watts or a Vietnam, all these universities are unstable.

* * *

The significance of the student revolt goes far beyond the
university; as far, in fact, as students can take it. Few radicals
would argue that the student revolt, all by itself, will usher
in a new era of revolutionary struggle. There may be more
students every year, but for a long time students will need
allies among other groups. Still fewer radicals would argue
that the university is *the* critical institution in advanced
countries and that bringing down the university would crip-
ple the system. The university may be increasingly important, but it's still just one among many institutions on the path
of the long march. What's important about the student revolt, and the French uprising for that matter, is not so much
what it *leads* to (who can tell?), but that it happened. Universities were supposed to be fairly stable institutions, well
integrated into their societies, which were also supposed to
be pretty stable. Even in Europe, where the university was
less than perfectly integrated, no one thought that its problems couldn't be solved by a few technical adjustments. Yet
both in Europe and the United States, it was precisely this
institution that cracked, spawning the first revolutionary left
movement the West has seen in two decades.

Leftists had gotten used to thinking of capitalism as the
doomed monolith of simple-minded Marxist mythology. As
its contradictions deepened into overt crises, capitalism
would stagger from crash to crash. For the great majority of
the working class, life would become steadily more miser-
able and oppressive until discontent ripened into massive rev-

olutionary consciousness. In fact, in the last thirty years, capitalism seems to have settled down to its golden (or at least plastic) age. Not that it has solved any of its problems. What it has learned is that contradictions can be covered with Band-Aids, crashes can be modulated into recessions, and rebellions can be levelled into disorders.

The disease that Marx diagnosed was still there under the cosmetics, but it seemed to have progressed from an acute to a chronic stage. Thus many leftists felt there was no possibility, at least for a while, of a revolutionary movement within an advanced capitalist country. The trouble would come from the periphery—from Vietnam, Bolivia, the Philippines, or the Congo. Today, after the May uprising in France, after the Springer riots, after Columbia and the battle of Valle Giulia, you can no longer write off the advanced capitalist countries. The student revolt occurred without the stimulus of a general crisis in capitalism or grossly oppressive conditions. What happened in the universities in the spring of 1968 can happen in other institutions, very much as it happened in the universities.

Underneath the layers of rationalizations, many institutions are fraught with absurdities and contradictions. It may be a long time before any of these contradictions come home to roost as a violent upheaval. Meanwhile, the people involved "contest inside themselves" (as a French student described his pre-May mood) with all kinds of tensions and ambivalences. Take an institution not far from the university—the public school. Most teachers enter their profession with the idea of teaching, only to discover that in many American schools, public education is essentially a clearing and holding operation. If you thought you were a teacher, but everyone else thinks you're an unarmed policeman, then you've got a lot more thinking to do.

Getting away from education, take a well-worn example from the annals of industrial sociology—the auto worker. No matter how mind-rotting the job is, he might like to think he is doing something useful, something worthy of a man's labor. But can he believe it as he drives home in his own car, through six lanes of almost motionless chrome? Finally, take an even more familiar example—the institutions of democracy. If you're over 25, you may have had the experience of voting for Johnson, to prevent a war in Vietnam. People who missed out on that come-down may have voted for Wallace—to restore the "little man" to a role in decision-making.

We could go on and on cataloging absurdities, but the examples are all trite. We're used to the idea of people doing one thing, and thinking they're doing something else, even *knowing* they're doing something else. Very few people crack up and fewer still become revolutionaries. Somehow most people manage to explain away or repress each inconsistency as an isolated or temporary aberration, without ever coming to question the whole system. According to psychologists, people are always trying to resolve their "cognitive dissonances," or reduce the level of discrepancy that they have to deal with. The most flagrant absurdities can be papered over with rationalizations.

But there are limits to this process of rationalization. A discrepancy can grow too wide to be bridged. Two or three small discrepancies can pile up all at once. Or something can happen that forces a person to confront ones that seemed safely buried. Then he may break—or he may accept the idea that the whole thing is irrational, and look for a new construction. This happens to individuals every day. When it happens to large groups, institutions are rocked; when it happens to masses of people, governments are overturned.

We know only one case well: what happened in the universities in the spring of 1968. Universities had plenty of obvious problems, especially in Europe, but none of them seemed insoluble. If student life wasn't altogether pleasurable, it was still far from intolerable. Deep down, of course, the university suffered from a grave contradiction—between the liberal, humanistic ethos it exuded and the work-a-day services for capitalism that it actually performed. But even this tension could be borne. Students were used to thinking critically for a term paper and thinking uncritically about what they were being trained for. If universities were completely insulated from the outside world, the conflict might never have surfaced. It took Vietnam for students to start wondering what they were going to be used for, to start asking if this was a society they really wanted a place in. It took business-directed university "reforms" for European students to ask who was training them, and what for.

Things piled up. There was Vietnam and the spectacle of racism in the United States. There was the draft. There was the university itself—boring, impersonal, repressive. There was the new youth culture presenting a living critique of how students lived and what they were supposed to become. These were cumulative influences. Each one unhinged a few more students. As some students became openly critical, then openly resistant, the discrepancies got harder and harder for the others to live with. It was a chain reaction within each university. When one university went, students were watching from dozens of others. The action spread from city to city and between continents in weeks. It happened so fast, with so little variation from country to country, that newspapers talked about a "conspiracy." They forgot that in every country the university tried to play the same role, suffered from the same contradictions, and used the same rationalizations. The same tinder was stacked up on campuses all over the world.

Of course, it didn't just happen. There is no such thing as the one dazzling insight that turns people into full-blown revolutionaries. In the university, many tiny confrontations preceded the mass rebellions. With every minor action, a few people were shaken loose from their old assumptions and rationalizations. Patient organizing and discussion cemented what people were beginning to put together from experience. With every new confrontation, it was easier to see how things *could* be. As the alternatives got clearer, the present system became more and more incredible and irrational. All this happened without there being any "objective" crises—other than those created by the struggle itself. Authoritarian institutions will not just collapse by themselves under the weight of their own contradictions. In confronting them, people make them unbelievable. As they become more unbelievable, they become more vulnerable to every assault.

If it can happen in the universities, it can happen in other institutions. And the university is more than an example. Universities are productive institutions: they produce people who go out into other institutions. They take in students, keep them together for a while, and then scatter them all through society. Students take with them what they've learned.

A Short Bibliography

A Short Bibliography

Germany

Kritische Universität, Sommer 68: Berichte und Program, AstA der Freien Universitat, 1 Berlin 33, Garystrasse 20. "Catalog" of the Berlin critical university.

U. Bergmann, R. Dutschke, W. Lefevre, and B. Rabehl, *Rebellion der Studenten,* Rowohlt. The story of the German movement as told by four leading participants.

L'Allemagne Fédérale après le Miracle, Partisans #41, March-April 1968. A collection, in French, of articles about Germany and the new German movement.

France

De la Misère en Milieu Étudiant, International Situationists. An English translation is available from Situationist International, P.O. Box 491, Cooper Station, New York, New York 10003. A widely influential situationist discussion of the position of students.

Paris: May 1968, Solidarity Pamphlet #30, c/o H. Russell, 53A Westmoreland Road, Bromley, Kent, England. An eyewitness account of the May events.

Première Histoire de la Révolution de Mai, L'événement, June 1968. An eyewitness account of the May events.

J. Sauvageot, A. Geismar, D. Cohn-Bendit, and J-P. Duteuil, *The French Student Revolt,* Hill and Wang. Four leading activists are interviewed on the May events.

Henri Lefebvre, *Explosion in France: The Meaning of the May Revolution,* Monthly Review Press, New York and London. An analysis of society, state, and ideology in the light of the French events by the noted French Marxist, professor of Sociology at Nanterre.

England

Ben Brewster and Alexander Cockburn, *Revolt at the LSE,* and G. S. Jones, A. Barnett, and T. Wengraf, *Student Power: What is to be Done,* New Left Review #43, May-June 1967.

David Adelstein, editor, *Teach Yourself Student Power,* mimeographed, Radical Students Alliance, c/o Students' Union, the Polytechnic, 19-21 Elsley Court, Great Titchfield Street, London W.1. Essays by English leftist students on university issues.

Columbia

James P. O'Brien, *The New Left's Early Years,* Radical America II, #3 (1968) (1237 Spaight St., Madison, Wisconsin).

Paul Jacobs and Saul Landau, *The New Radicals,* Vintage.

Who Rules Columbia, North American Congress on Latin America, P.O. Box 57, Cathedral Park Station, New York, N.Y. 10025. A detailed discussion of the leaders and activities of Columbia University.

Columbia Liberated, revised edition, Columbia Strike Coordinating Committee, available from Peter Clapp, 501 W. 110th St., Apt. 7E, New York, New York. The Columbia events, from the Strike Committee's side.

Conclusion

Jerry Farber, "The Student, as Nigger," from *This Magazine is About Schools,* available from Radical Education Project, Box 625, Ann Arbor, Michigan 48107. On the repressive functions of the American university.

Carl Davidson, *The Multiversity: Crucible of the New Working Class,* available from S.D.S., 1608 West Madison, Chicago, Illinois 60612. The new role of the university and resulting strategic consideration for the Left.

Viet Report: Special Issue on the University and the Military, available from Radical Education Project, Box 625, Ann Arbor, Michigan 48107. Names the names, tells the tales of the university-military alliance.

Books that have had a major impact on student activists

Paul Baran and Paul Sweezy, *Monopoly Capital*, Monthly Review Press.

Che Guevara, *Guerrilla Warfare*, Monthly Review Press.

Malcolm X, *The Autobiography of Malcolm X*, Grove Press.

Mao Tse Tung, *The Little Red Book*

Karl Marx, *The Communist Manifesto*

Herbert Marcuse, *Eros and Civilization*, Vintage Books.

————, *One-Dimensional Man*, Beacon Press.

Wilhelm Reich, *The Sexual Revolution*, Noonday Press.